THE
GARDEN IN FLOWER
month-by-month

THE
GARDEN IN FLOWER

month-by-month

JOHN KELLY

Photographs by John Kelly

David & Charles

For my godson, Robin Cameron Aggleton, whose mother taught me this:

June – too soon
July – they'll try
August – come they must
September – remember!
October – all over.

Traditional Caribbean rhyme for predicting hurricanes . . .

. . . it is equally applicable to the flowering of hydrangeas.

Flower Garden

A DAVID & CHARLES BOOK

Copyright © John Kelly 1994
Photographs © John Kelly 1994

First published 1994
First paperback edition 1997

John Kelly has asserted his right to be identified as author of this
work in accordance with the Copyright, Designs and Patents Act
1988.

A catalogue record for this book is available from the British
Library.

ISBN 0 7153 0076 8 hardback
ISBN 0 7153 0568 9 paperback

Book design by Diana Knapp
Illustrations by Avis Murray
Typeset by ABM Typographics Ltd, Hull
and printed in Italy
by New Interlitho SpA
for David & Charles
Brunel House Newton Abbot Devon

CONTENTS

INTRODUCTION

If you have the good fortune to live in a part of the world where the climate is cool-temperate and reasonably equable, gardening is a wide-open book of delights from which you can make an almost limitless choice of flowering plants. The permutations of plant associations and combinations are also virtually infinite – here is an unparalleled medium of self-expression.

Even if the chill fingers of a continental winter are apt to reach out and envelop your garden, or if the stalking figure of drought is wont to blight your summer, there is still a wealth of possibility in flower gardening. Gardeners are ingenious if nothing else, and it is always a pleasure to see a rock garden in the Arizona desert, Mexican dahlias in a Limerick rainscape, and Californian ceanothus like patches of fallen sky in Dorset or Cambridge.

Old habits die hard, however, and it is still commonplace to see gardens dedicated to only one month of the year and there may be a crocus or two here and there as a sop to the rest of the year. All too often the summer border and the spring garden rule – although it has to be admitted that they do so less now than a few decades ago – and the rest of the year merely serves as preparation for the two climaxes.

Paradoxically, this is precisely because the choice is so wide. Gardens are finite areas, and the space for flowering plants within them is often governed by factors other than the merely horticultural. Children must have somewhere safe and pleasant to play; adults need such things as fuel stores, washing lines, compost heaps, vegetable gardens, and somewhere comfortable to sit and enjoy an evening drink or a barbecue.

Given a minute patch of earth in which

to plant flowering plants, and faced with a huge range of shrubs, perennials and bulbs, not to mention trees, from which to choose, it is not surprising that we tend to think 'summer' or 'spring' and go for broke. How can you possibly wade through all the garden literature and sort out a succession of flowering plants that will keep the garden reasonably colourful for nine, if not twelve of the months of the year? To do the necessary research means trawling for information about flowering times from a score of sources and then making some sort of chart, from which you then make your choice. The task would be a hard one for a full-time researcher, let alone someone who has to go to work, take the children to school, cook meals, clean houses, chair committees, entertain business contacts, bone up on tomorrow's history seminar, or whatever among the countless demands on one's time fall to your particular lot.

This book does not substitute for that work. What it does is collate enough information to set your feet upon the path of a balanced flowering garden, one in which there will be colour and interest every day of the year, and which will not have one or even two mighty explosions of flamboyance, but a steady output of harmony and grace.

No garden book, no matter how weighty and comprehensive a work it is or may claim to be, should ever set itself up as the answer to the seeking for perfection in which all good gardeners indulge. This one does not tell you all in one go how to have the garden to end all gardens. Its aim is to encourage experiment and the study of catalogues, and to enjoin you to approach your garden planning and planting with a wide-open and receptive eye. Its purpose is to nudge you towards

SEASONS AND MONTHS

Under average conditions, the terms 'early', 'mid' and 'late' season are used throughout this book to correspond to the following months:

SPRING
Early: March
Mid: April
Late: May

SUMMER
Early: June
Mid: July
Late: August

AUTUMN
Early: September
Mid: October
Late: November

WINTER
Early: December
Mid: January
Late: February

(opposite) At the height of summer, hydrangeas begin their long flowering season. H. macrophylla 'Mme A. Riverain' among agapanthus

gaining and using experience in a field in which a nudge is certainly essential.

It goes without saying that the attainment of a well-ordered garden of any sort is impossible without a grasp of the fundamentals of the practical side of gardening. If you do not understand how to prune without cutting away the season's flowers; suffer failure year in year out with sowing seeds of anything beyond the easiest annuals; cannot make a garden pond without its leaking, becoming choked with green slime and killing every living thing within it; and do not know how to make a piece of stem grow roots and evolve into a new plant, your gardening experience will be unsatisfactory, disappointing and probably boring.

Therefore, you will find here some guidance towards various practices, methods and techniques that will assist you in providing a home for an ever-increasing wealth of flowering plants. Stocking a garden is an expensive business. You have only to go to the garden centre and buy fifty assorted trees, shrubs and perennials to have spent the average weekly industrial wage. It is undoubtedly money well spent, and you will probably contemplate such levels of outlay for the framework of the plantings. But in order to have a really fine display of flowers throughout the year, you will find the need to propagate plants yourself almost overwhelming.

For this reason, I have devoted space to the techniques and equipment involved in propagating the widest possible range of flowering plants. You may think a mist propagation unit an extravagance, but just extrapolate from the figure I have given you above and you will realise that, far from being a luxury, it is something approaching a necessity.

Throughout the book I emphasise the concept of foresight, and extol it as the ultimate virtue in a gardener. At the FBI's Academy at Quantico, Virginia, they teach the six Ps (there are seven, but I have left one out for propriety) thus: Proper Prior Planning Prevents Poor Performance. It should be flown as a banner above every potting shed in the gardening world. Good gardening of any kind is impossible without good planning. When it comes to arranging for flowers to appear all year

round without robbing summer's glory or demoting spring from its magical ascendancy, to fail to plan is to assure total failure.

Planning is one of the boring concepts like 'book-keeping' and 'doing the tax return', but it has been invested with its dullness by dull people. Planning a garden is quite the most enjoyable pastime I can think of, other than sitting in a Kenmare pub with a pint of black stout or watching the Cincinnati Reds win a World Series. It involves far more than sitting morosely over a piece of squared paper. It requires the investigative talents of Miss Marple, the cheek of a door-to-door salesman, and an appreciation of the fact that to steal ideas from one garden is plagiarism, but to steal them from several is research.

For planning means, among other things, going and looking at other gardens. Let me give you examples, drawn from my own garden-planning forays. I have studied the underplanting of roses at the home of the Royal National Rose Society, how to make the most of late winter bulbs at the Royal Horticultural Society's garden at Wisley, how to plant colourfully where the daffodils were flowering from my sister-in-law in Sussex, the best ways of deploying camellias from Leu Gardens in downtown Orlando, and how to make the most of water-lilies from a garden in Mombasa, Kenya. And that is a tiny fraction of the research I have done in garden planning. During the course of my career I have visited countless gardens, from the tiny to the grandiose, and learned something important from every single one.

To all the owners and operators of all those gardens I am exceedingly grateful, and you will be grateful to those whose gardens you may visit in the search for ideas for flowering plants to brighten the months that are usually on the dull side.

The more mundane aspect of planning involves looking constantly ahead. The times for choosing, planting and for flowers to appear rarely coincide. When they do it is usually during late spring or that part of the summer holidays that comes before the children's school uniforms have to be bought, which is one of the reasons for the burgeoning of gardens at those times. That bulb plantings are so often haphazard or thoroughly inappropriate is often because choosing and plant-

ing take place in autumn, while flowering happens in spring, fully six months or even more afterwards. To go and see bulbs in flower, notebook in hand, in a garden where they are labelled or where the owner knows their names, is an essential adjunct to good choice. Catalogue colours are often inaccurate and verbal descriptions (apart from mine, of course) not to be relied upon.

It is one thing to plant so as to achieve colour and interest throughout the year, quite another to ensure that your plantings will be harmonious. I am, in general, loath to give too many concrete examples or to draw too many planting plans, as I believe they can be restrictive. I would far rather succeed in inculcating the general principles of colour association than see any plan of mine rendered plant for plant. With the vast choice of plants that is available to us, the chances for self expression are legion, as long as such ideas as proper tonal order are adhered to. If you always try to combine a light tone of a light colour with a dark tone of a dark colour, rather than the other way round, it will be infinitely more worthwhile than executing a specific example.

Nevertheless, certain points are made more expressly by the use of examples, and where they serve a purpose I have given them. However, I would like to emphasise that they are only illustrations, and that your own plant associations and combinations stand a good chance of being better than mine.

There is an influential school that decrees that pastel colours are *de rigueur* in gardening and that strong, clear, even raw hues are in 'bad taste'. It is founded upon a fear and lack of understanding of colour, and has unfortunately acquired guru status. Its logical extension into retreat from colour is the white garden – a pity, as a drift of white flowers lightened by just one touch of another colour creates one of the most telling effects of all.

The pastel garden is a garden that misses the point. It denies the joyousness of nature and relegates to 'bad taste' the works of the Almighty. Of course, colour is easily deployed in ways that shock or offend those with sensitive aesthetic perceptions – and sometimes they do not have to be so sensitive. But to be so offensive as

to dismiss as bad taste the love and attention that have gone into a garden is unforgiveable. By all means be as bold as you like, use fierce orange and satanic red; let vivid purple add a royal touch to your plantings, enjoy near-black hellebores if you like them and do not eschew green flowers if you find them fascinating. Garden for you and yours, and not for the censorious passer-by.

The love of flowers is deep in the heredity of all of us. The world we came into as primitive beings many thousands of years ago knew colour only through nature, and the most colourful things in nature were the flowers. This book will, I hope, help you to surround yourself with flowers for as much of the year as your climate allows. If the result is a deepening of your gardening perceptions and pleasure, it will not have been written in vain.

USING THE BOOK

This book is divided into months so that practical information is quickly accessible to the gardener at any time of the year. If, for example, you want to check that you have done all the necessary routine jobs in the garden in a particular month, simply turn to the appropriate maintenance section. Plant Profiles for each month list a selection of the most attractive plants in flower for that month; the Plants in Flower section provides a more comprehensive list with, necessarily, less information about individual plants – the aim is to give the reader an idea of the wealth of choice available. Other sections in each month tell you how to propagate, how to plan and plant so that you have an attractive garden all year round. Finally there are suggestions for practical projects to improve your garden, or your gardening.

For ease of use the book is divided into twelve months, or sections. However, flowering periods vary greatly depending on weather conditions so more general terms, for example mid-spring and late autumn, are used, allowing the gardener, who is more used to his or her own area, to judge when projects and planting are best undertaken. The table on page 7 is a guide to the average conditions.

LISTS AND TABLES OF PLANTS IN FLOWER

The best way to use the lists and tables for any given month is to read them in conjunction with those for the months before and after. This will give a broader picture upon which you can with some realism base your gardening plans.

The lists of plants for each month are meant to be a guide and are neither comprehensive nor precise. Comprehensiveness is prohibited by reasons of space; precision by the ways of nature.

The flowering times of plants are highly variable, especially in winter and spring. The factors governing flowering time are the prevailing climate (continental, maritime, etc), the local climate, microclimates, altitude, soil (heavy soils are late, light ones are early), the strength of the light (governed in turn by climate and latitude) and often the age of the plant.

The length of the flowering season of a given plant varies also, but it is often cultural conditions that determine for how long a plant will bloom.

In addition to these factors, there are others that are imperfectly understood, either by your author or by science. An example of the variability of flowering is that of *Pieris* 'Taiwanensis', which is usually cited as flowering in the British Isles in April. In fact, it can start flowering at the end of January in the south-west of Ireland, to finish in mid-March, or it can begin in May in the northern parts of Scotland, where its season is shorter and it is likely to finish in the same month. In the United States of America, the same shrub will flower at radically different times in the mild, maritime climate of much of Washington and Oregon, and the colder, continentally-dominated climate of upper New York State (where it would be likely to need winter protection).

Many plants flower in more than one month. To have included every plant flowering in every month would have made demands on space that I could not have met, and I have omitted plants from those months during which, although they may be very nearly in full flower, they are not at their peak – given the provisos above.

Thus, from the lists early summer appears to be as good a time for shrub flowering as midsummer, which is not the case. Many shrubs that are at their best in early summer also flower in midsummer, and space does not allow their being mentioned there.

Bright and bold Dianthus *'Sweet Beauty' and* Lychnis chalcedonica *combine with* Nepeta *'Six Hills Giant' apparently flouting conventional colour-matching*

J A N U A R Y

The English winter – ending in July,
To recommence in August
BYRON

*Well, he would say that, wouldn't he, a man who was never
happy unless by the shores of the warm Aegean. If he had stayed
around long enough he would have realised that the English
winter seems long only because it is so mild. Autumn, winter and
spring are merely variations on a theme when compared with the
difference between August and January in New York or Boston.
The colder months have subtle differences between them, to discern
which my Lord Byron appears to have lacked the patience. This
month is colder than last, but the days are gradually lengthening,
not much, but enough to trigger certain plants – the earliest irises,
the very first spring crocuses, winter aconites and snowdrops –
into bloom. Its milder spells will, with increasing certainty, tempt
hamamelis, winter-flowering cherry, wintersweet and Christmas
box into flower, and release the fragrances of viburnums.*
*Now is the beginning of the end of winter – the first Act of the
year's drama truly begins. This month it is not yet curtain up, but
time for the overture. It starts quietly, with a tentative theme that
passes through its variations with increasing confidence until, by
the month's end, there is a hint, if not of merriment, then of relief
that the worst is over. Next month can see a return to the
bleakness, but never the blackness of the depths of winter.
It is at this time of year that a gardener's spirit proves its worth.
In his or her mind's eye there is no longer the gloom of winter,
there is a soaring picture of perfect borders to be achieved,
blossoms generously falling to paths below, luscious scents and
birdsong. Oh, cynical Byron! If only you had listened to
Wordsworth!*

tasks

FOR THE

month

1

PREPARE FOR HARDY ANNUALS
In a dry spell, prepare the ground for early-spring sowings of hardy annuals. Dig the sites over, removing any perennial weed seeds, and incorporate organic matter such as peat or garden compost.

MANURE VERSUS BONEMEAL
Now is the time to top dress roses with either well-rotted manure or bonemeal, but not both at the same time. They react together, driving off the nitrates in the manure as ammonia gas.

WOODY WASTE
Any bits of twig, prunings you failed to pick up, or any woody debris at all, can all too readily set up infections of coral spot fungus. In no time, it can destroy your favourite tree. Burn them.

CHECKLIST

- As bulbs emerge, rake gently among them with a hand fork to break up and aerate capped soil
- Check your hardwood cuttings. If they have been disturbed by frost, firm them back
- Continue to plant trees and shrubs in open weather
- Continue pruning deciduous shrubs and trees and pay special care to removing all dead wood. Return to Japanese maples later, at leaf-break, and head back branchlets whose tips have died back
- You can still plant roses if necessary
- Protect crocus flowers from mud splash by mulching the area with a fine grade of composted forest bark
- You can plant winter-flowering heathers now if you like, to give some instant colour, but aim to plan better in future. Foresight is characteristic of the better gardener
- Make plans for planning a mixed border

PLANTING

PLANTING DISTANCES

Read the plant-buyer's guide on page 19 to save you a great deal of work in winters to come. Then follow these planting guidelines. No matter how small the specimen you fondly carry home, plant according to the best information you have.

When it comes to width, or crown spread, in trees and shrubs, take care that you do not make the extremely common mistake of planting so that the centres of the plants are separated by the amounts of their spreads only. For example, if you buy two shrubs whose spreads after ten years will be 2m (7ft) each, do not plant them

2m (7ft) apart (ie at 2m (7ft) centres). If you do and they grow the slightest bit more than that – as they will, one supposes, in year eleven – they will grow into one another and become misshapen.

Always allow for more than the ten-year spread. If I am planting shrubs whose spreads are likely to be 2m (7ft), I allow half that distance as the ten-year gap between them. When planting shrubs of differing spreads, I allow half the spread of the larger shrub as the gap.

The way you will save winter work is in not having to move shrubs that have become overcrowded. This is the most usual and the most easily avoided reason for transplanting semi-mature shrubs and trees.

PLANNING

THE MIXED BORDER

The above shows that it is not a good ambition to have a shrub border in the strict sense. When the young shrubs are planted there will be large distances between them, and there should still be significant gaps after a decade. These areas should be rendered unrecognisable as mere gaps between shrubs by your planting perennials, which can easily be reduced in number as the shrubs grow, whereas the shrubs cannot be reduced in size without ruining them. Close to the roots of the shrubs you should grow annuals such as nicotianas, which can be sown in situ and removed without disturbance. Bulbs, too can be planted among the shrubs.

What you will have created, in short, is a mixed border, and it is this towards which your ambitions should be directed. If it is, you will find yourself planning it as a whole, so that the colours and shapes of the flowers of the shrubs harmonise with those of the perennials, annuals and bulbs, and everything is in balance and there is none of the distortion, darkness and disease so common among shrub plantings.

PROPAGATION

ROOT CUTTINGS

Many perennial plants and just a few shrubs are better propagated from root cuttings than by any other method. There are many reasons for this. With border phloxes, particularly varieties of *Phlox paniculata*, it

PLANTING DISTANCES

Incorrect – after 10 years

Correct – after 10 years

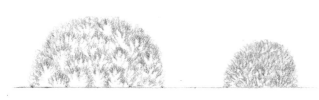

Correct spacing for shrubs of different spreads

is the only certain way of producing plants free of eelworm. *Geranium* 'Ballerina', a highly popular rock-garden plant, is one of a group of geraniums that make little stem-cuttings material and cannot be divided. From root cuttings a good increase can be obtained.

This is the best month for taking root cuttings, as the plants are dormant and will not suffer from loss of a proportion of their root systems. Of course, if a large number of cuttings are taken from a plant, it will die, so you take either a few and keep the parent going, or many and do away with it.

■ Lift the plant with the root system as intact as you can and wash the soil away from part of it. You will find that the plants mentioned above will have long, thick roots with a consistency somewhere between woody and fleshy. Look for one the thickness of a pencil – from diary pencil to regular desk model. Cut it off, making a horizontal cut, and unravel it from the rest of the system.

■ Now cut it into sections 3-5cm (1¼–2in) long, each time cutting with a horizontal cut. Immediately you have severed a cutting, re-cut the bottom with a slanting cut. In this way you will always know which way is up.

■ There are two ways of setting the cuttings. With slender, malleable ones, such as are obtained from phloxes, lay them lengthwise on the surface of a 50/50 mixture by volume of sharp sand and moss peat in a pot, and cover them only 1cm (½in) deep, firming the compost down onto them.

Other, stouter cuttings may be inserted vertically into the compost so that their tops are just covered. It is for these that the difference between top and bottom is vital: an upside-down root cutting will never root.

■ Whichever method you use, put the pot in a cold greenhouse or frame, water it well, and keep it moist but not wet. In spring, you will see little green buttons on the surface, and these rapidly grow into new shoots.

■ Where most people fail with root cuttings is in disturbing them too early. The shoots develop before the new roots and live for a while on the food reserves in the cuttings. Moving them at this stage will inhibit root development. Allow the shoots to grow on well and then tap out the contents of the pot. Gently separate the newly rooted plants and, with great care, pot them up.

Root hairs, the organs that do the actual job of absorbing water and inorganic salts from the soil, are one cell thick and invisible. One single cubic inch of soil may contain as much as six thousand miles of root hairs. If you damage many of those newly formed on a root cutting you lessen its chances of establishment, but by not being too hasty you increase them many hundredfold.

PLANTS FOR ROOT CUTTINGS

Acanthus
Aesculus parviflora
Ailanthus
Anchusa
Arnebia
Brunnera
Campsis
Carduncellus
Centaurea (some)
Clerodendrum
Convolvulus
Crambe
Dicentra
Echinacea
Echinops
Erodium
Gaillardia
Halesia
Japanese anemone
Limonium
Morisia
Papaver orientale (oriental poppy)
Primula denticulata
Rhus
Romneya
Verbascum

plants
OF THE
month

IRIS
Iris unguicularis (syn. *Iris stylosa*)

The Algerian iris is one of the most surprising of plants. It is bone hardy, which is strange for a plant from North Africa, its flowers are un- usually large for one that blooms in winter, its winter flowering itself is a surprise, and it lives practically on nothing. Its beauty is little short of astonishing.

type	Evergreen perennial
flowers	Typical of a beardless iris. Lilac- lavender and pinkish-lavender forms are the earliest flowering. Darker, purple forms such as 'Mary Barnard', rarely flower before spring. Lightly fragrant. Midwinter to early spring
foliage	Grassy
height	The plant's height is in its leaves. Ideally it should be not much more than 30cm (1ft), but when fed rather too well it can be twice that and liable to hide the flowers
spread	60cm (2ft)
hardiness	Hardy
planting	Plant from a pot at any time, otherwise in late summer to early autumn
position	Hot and dry, preferably at the foot of a sunny wall
soil	Poor, preferably limy and rubbly. Do not feed. Richer conditions encourage leaves at the expense of flowers
propagation	By division of established clumps in late summer or early autumn if dry conditions persist
varieties	'Walter Butt' is early and free flowering, but the flower shape is not very good. There is a white form. *Iris lazica* is a similar species with broader leaves flowering later in the winter. Its flowers are a good violet-blue

WINTER ACONITE
Eranthis hyemalis

The common winter aconite flowers towards the end of the month in warmer parts, a little later where it is cooler. It naturalises freely in leafy places beneath trees, and is highly valued for its yellow flowers at a time of year when most at ground level are in the lilac to lavender range.

type	Tuberous perennial
flowers	Buttercup-like, rich yellow
foliage	Basal, much divided. The 'leaves' below the flowers are bracts
height	8cm (3in)
spread	Colonises
hardiness	Hardy
planting	Plant when available
position	Full or part shade. It should be left alone to naturalise
soil	Leafy
propagation	By lifting self-sown tubers
alternatives	*E. × tubergenii* is a larger plant but it does not self-seed. *E. × t.* 'Guinea Gold' has deep yellow flowers with bronze tints and is a little later

WITCH HAZEL
Hamamelis mollis 'Pallida'

This is possibly the most popular of the witch hazels. It flowers very freely, with its naked branches wreathed in clusters of curious, spidery flowers. Their scent is not heavy and sickly, as in some others, but is a strong and yet delicate fragrance. It may flower at any time between early winter and early spring, but is usually at its best towards the end of this month. Its leaves turn rich, butter-yellow in autumn.

IRIS UNGUICULARIS

CROCUS TOMASINIANUS

type	Deciduous shrub
flowers	Lemon yellow
foliage	Wide, hazel-like
height	2m (7ft) after 10 years
spread	1.8m (6ft)
hardiness	Hardy
position	Sun or part shade
soil	Any good garden soil
pruning	None
propagation	By layering in midsummer or spliced side-veneer grafting (see p.154) onto *Hamamelis virginiana* seedlings in spring. Seeds of the other species are decidedly reluctant to germinate, even when sown as soon as ripe. I have had little success with cuttings of any kind, even under mist
alternatives	*H.m.* 'Brevipetala' has orange-yellow, short-petalled flowers with a heavy scent. 'Coombe Wood' has darker yellow flowers and a fine scent

CROCUS

Crocus tomasinianus hybrid

There are several forms of the 'Tommy' crocus. Some are very free-seeding and crop up all over the place, others just quietly get on with establishing themselves in rapidly increasing clumps. An occasional flower may suffer the attentions of an inquisitive creature looking for nectar, but among so many it makes hardly a difference. The true species is now considered unobtainable and all corms offered are really hybrids. *Crocus tomasinianus* is quite the most cheekily cheerful of plants and a great companion on a fresh, sunny day later in the month.

type	Corm
flowers	Vary from purple-lilac and reddish purple to mauvish blue, occasionally white
foliage	Grassy, flowers and foliage borne together
height	8cm (3in)
spread	Spreads by seeding
hardiness	Hardy
planting	Plant in autumn
position	Almost anywhere
soil	Almost any
propagation	By lifting naturalised corms when dormant
varieties	Crocuses under the name of the species and given names such as 'Albus', 'Rose', 'Ruby Giant' and 'Whitewell Purple' are excellent propositions. The latter two are ideal for naturalising

plants
IN
flower

ROCK GARDEN

The main flowers on the rock garden will be
among the bulbs listed right

ORNAMENTAL BARK AND TWIGS

When there are few flowers in the garden, it is not
just berries and autumn foliage that can provide
the missing colour. Deciduous trees and shrubs
with beautiful bark are invaluable this month and
next, when most berries have gone and deciduous
trees and shrubs are leafless. The list on the right
is a selection only; it is not comprehensive.

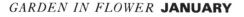

SHRUBS	colour	flower type
Camellia sasanqua 'Narumi-gata'	White	Small, single, fragrant
'Crimson King'	Red	Small, single
Chimonanthus praecox (Wintersweet)	Pale yellow	Very fragrant
Garrya elliptica	Greenish	Tassels
Sarcococca spp (Christmas box)	White	Small, highly scented

Also: **Erica carnea, Erica × darleyensis, Hamamelis** (many vars), **Jasminum nudiflorum, Lonicera fragrantissimum, L. × purpusii, L. standishii, Viburnum × bodnantense, V. farreri, V. tinus.**

PERENNIALS	colour	height
Iris unguicularis	Lilac-lavender	30cm (12in)

CLIMBERS		
Clematis cirrhosa balearica (Fern-leaved clematis)	Pale yellow, red spots	

BULBS		
Crocus ancyrensis	Orange-yellow	5cm (2in)
imperati	Violet inside, buff outside	10cm (4in)
tomasinianus	Lavender or pink	10cm (4in)
Eranthis hyemalis	Yellow	8cm (3in)
Galanthus graecus	White, green markings	10cm (4in)
Iris danfordiae	Lemon yellow	12cm (5in)
histrioides major	Royal blue, white and gold markings	10cm (4in)
'Katherine Hodgkin'	Cream, overlaid with pale yellow and blue	10cm (4in)

Also: **Cyclamen coum** aggregate.

TREES for ornamental twigs and bark	
Acer davidii	Red 'snake-bark', marked snakeskin fashion with white
griseum	Mahogany orange, peeling bark
grosseri var. *hersii*	Snake-bark marbling
pensylvanicum	Snake-bark maple in green and white
Betula albo-sinensis var. *septentrionalis*	Peeling bark in soft, fawnish pink
utilis var. *jacquemontii*	White
papyrifera	White, peeling
pendula	Silver birch

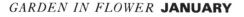

***Eucalyptus* spp**	*Many different kinds: flaking, peeling, in blue, blue-grey, green-grey, cream and combinations of these*
Prunus serrula	*Bright mahogany, glossy*
Salix daphnoides	*Violet with a white 'bloom'*
irrorata	*'Purple with a white 'bloom'. Sometimes a shrub*
alba 'Britzensis'	*Brilliant orange-scarlet branches. Prune hard every other year*

SHRUBS for ornamental twigs and bark

***Acer palmatum* 'Senkaki'**	*Brilliant coral red twigs and branches*
***Arbutus andrachne**	*Cinnamon brown*
Cornus (European) – several kinds	*Bright red or yellow. Stool every other spring*
Leycesteria formosa	*Green stems*
***Myrtus luma**	*Cinnamon orange, peeling*
Parrotia persica	*Flaking stems like old iron. Sometimes a tree*
***Rhododendron thomsonii**	*Deep, glowing crimson main stems*
Rubus cockburnianus	*Arching stems appear as if whitewashed*

THINK OF AUTUMN

Plant *Rosa moyesii,* which has long, erect-arching, clean branches, near to *Acer griseum.* The brilliant red flowers are beautiful in their own right, but the large, long-lasting hips, like upside-down, sealing-wax-red amphorae, are unbelievably gorgeous in combination firstly with the tree's daring, coal-fire-at-bedtime autumn colour, and then with the peeling, mahogany bark, whose flakes are bright orange with the sun behind them.

A PLANT-BUYER'S GUIDE

The days of the altruistic nurseryman are gone. No longer can you expect universally to hear the truth when you ask questions about plants. Many people in the trade, though perhaps well-trained in horticulture, work for enterprises that are, like so many today, ruled by accountants. If they wish to keep their jobs, they must sell. This is not universally so, but enough that you should wear a sceptical garment when buying trees, shrubs and perennials.

Here are the rules for the well-informed plant buyer:

■ *Never ask how tall a tree or shrub grows. You will be told 'Not very big', or 'Oh, it takes ages to get to any size'. If, on the other hand, the salesman spots that you really do want a large tree, his tune will change. Always ask, 'How tall will this shrub/tree become ten years from now?' If he does not know, or does not find out, go elsewhere.*

■ *Adopt the same approach concerning the spread of the tree or shrub, but be specific: 'How wide will the crown or head of branches become in ten years from now?' Spread, when applied to herbaceous plants, means the span of the plant when in leaf: take care that you are not told the width of its crown, which is at ground level and much narrower.*

■ *Never ask in what conditions a plant will grow: always ask in what conditions it will* not *grow. The question, 'Will it grow in my conditions' expects the answer 'Yes', and will probably get it. 'Tell me what soils and situations it does not like' forces the salesman to tell the truth.*

■ *Never dismiss a salesman who admits to lack of knowledge. However, if he makes not the slightest move towards finding out the answers to your questions, go elsewhere.*

■ *Never ask, 'Is this plant hardy?' Again, it expects the answer 'Yes'. If the nursery or garden centre is local, ask instead, 'Will this plant stand the worst winters round here?' If you are far from home ask if it will stand the worst winters in exposed conditions in the south/east/north or wherever you live.*

■ *Never buy a 'dwarf' or 'slow-growing' conifer without either looking it up in a good book or asking a nurseryman whom you trust how large it will become after ten years. In the less scrupulous areas of the trade 'slow-growing' conifers become forest trees with remarkable speed and 'dwarf' ones are merely slow growing.*

■ *Gardening is* not *a trade into which dim children are sent as a last resort. People buying plants can be extraordinarily rude and patronising, usually, one hopes, without meaning to be. Get the sales person on your side and you will come away with better information.*

FEBRUARY

Here comes February, a little girl with her
first valentine, a red bow in her wind-blown
hair, a kiss waiting on her lips, a tantrum
just back of her laughter.

HAL BORLAND
(1964)

This month can charm you with sunshine as strong as that of
᷍umn, it can freeze the falling rain into terrible ice, it is
᷍ly capable of gales of hurricane force, and it can bury all
thoughts of gardening beneath a duvet of snow.

Gen᷍ ly, in those parts of the world where gardening is usually
possib᷍ now, it is not as wet as in late autumn and early winter.
Yet, like the little girl with a curl in the middle of her forehead,
this month, when very bad, can be horrid. It can rain, in an off
year, as if the future of the world depended on it. Then it becomes
'February fill-dyke' (Thomas Tusser c.1564), and you should
resolutely stay off the soil and keep to the paths – or the armchair
– until the fit passes.

The flowers that brave all this are equipped with hardiness of
quite astonishing proportions. Crocuses will stand under water
for days at a time and then open as if nothing had happened. The
reticulata irises, brave enough in any case at this time of year,
surpass themselves in courage and beauty when thrusting their
indomitable flowers through snow. And snowdrops take
everything that comes, nod sagely, and carry on as if to aver that
a few million years of evolution have taught them that this is
nothing, really.

Overhead, some shrubs and a few trees keep up the continuo to the
overture to spring. They bear the flowers of winter and have done
so for some time now, off and on. Soon, however, their final
chord will die away, the opening fanfare of true spring will
sound, and Act I of the gardening year will commence once again.
As Marcus Aurelius said, all things from eternity . . . come round
in a circle.

tasks
FOR THE
month
1

CHECKLIST

- ☐ Sow seeds of trees and shrubs under glass
- ☐ Sow seeds of alpines in a garden frame
- ☐ This is the last month during which you can safely plant out bare-rooted roses
- ☐ Lilies may be transplanted towards the end of this month in milder districts. Be careful to keep as much soil round them as possible
- ☐ Go round coloured-leaved shrubs such as *Spiraea* 'Gold Flame', removing any green, reverted shoots
- ☐ Plant clematis
- ☐ Prune late-flowering, large-flowered clematis and hydrangeas
- ☐ Remove suckers from roses
- ☐ Order summer-flowering bulbs, such as galtonias, gladioli and crinums
- ☐ *Buddleia davidii* varieties may be pruned hard back now, but in colder areas leave until next month

MAINTENANCE

PRUNING CLEMATIS

There is more confusion over this one small facet of gardening than almost any other.

Clematis are natural climbers of trees and large shrubs. With the exception of alpine species, it is of no advantage to them to produce leaves and flowers all along their stems, as it is only at the ends that they will be in sun; the greater part of the stems are hidden among the leaves of the host tree.

Gardeners, however, require flowers from near ground level upwards. To achieve that, they have to ensure a framework of the sorts of stems that do flower. These are either (A) produced on short growths from the wood of the previous year, or (B) on the growth of the current year.

Group A clematis should have previously flowered, dead growths removed; this should really have been done last autumn but can be done now. Growths made last year may be cut back to a strong pair of buds, thus diverting energy into all the leaf axils from which flower stems will be made. This pruning is *not* essential, just advisable. Old, tangled plants may be pruned to within 30cm (1ft) of the ground, but you will lose the flowers for that particular year.

Group B clematis should have the entire head of branches made last year removed, as you are only interested in the new growth that will flower this year. Prune all growths back to within 30cm (1ft) of the ground. This pruning *is* essential.

You can tell Group A from Group B thus:

● Group A clematis flower in late spring to early summer, and then again in early to mid-autumn.

● Group B clematis do not start flowering before midsummer.

● Group C consists of species clematis that produce their flowers before the end of spring, including *C. montana, alpina* and *C. macropetala.* The only pruning required is the removal of weak or dead stems.

NOTE

● *Please note that it is an excellent idea to grow large-flowered clematis into trees and over large shrubs. The logic of the above paragraphs demonstrates that they should not be pruned at all* ■

Hearty growers among the species, such as *C. orientalis,* may be thinned as needed. The winter-flowering *C. cirrhosa balearica* need

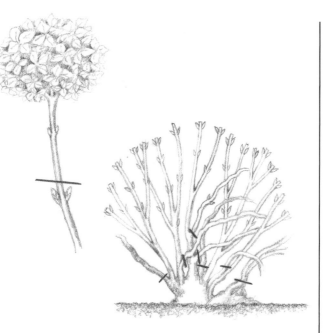

not be pruned if it is allowed to do its job of covering dead trees or old walls.

PRUNING HYDRANGEAS

Hydrangeas may be pruned later this month and into next.

H. macrophylla varieties, which include all the 'mopheads' and 'lacecaps' – in other words the best-known hydrangeas – are easily pruned incorrectly. This is the correct way:

■ Firstly, go over each bush and remove the dead flowerheads, cutting each stem back to the first strong pair of buds below the head. You should not have done this earlier, as the old flowerheads afford an important measure of frost protection.

■ Now go down to the very bottom of the bush and remove as close to ground level as possible all growths that are old, gnarled, weak, badly crossing or diseased. With a bush that has not been pruned for years, you may need to do this in two or even three annual 'bites'. This will encourage the production from the base of straight, strong, rapid shoots that will flower the same summer.

■ Even well-grown hydrangeas should have some of the older growths removed each year once they have become established, otherwise flowering will gradually decline.

PLANNING

SCENT

Scented plants are often planted with little thought to how the scent is best to be appreciated. It is little use, for example, going to the trouble of seeking out shrubs with scented flowers and then planting them on the eastern boundary of the garden when the prevailing wind is westerly.

Equally, it makes poor sense to plant shrubs with winter scent anywhere but near a path. The last thing you want to do is to have to plunge through mud, snow and dripping branches to take a sniff of a pleasant perfume; you are more than likely not to bother.

Although a few plants have scents that do not waft on the air and demand that you approach them closely, the majority are better appreciated when they take you by surprise. A garden is by definition a contrived place, and its surprises are therefore planned, but that does not reduce the surprise value of scents. It is physiologically impossible consciously to remember a scent. We think we remember them, but in fact recall only that they were pleasant or unpleasant. Each time a scent is encountered, it has about it a degree of novelty, even though it may recall with great vividness a partly forgotten episode in one's life.

You can, therefore, deliberately plan to surprise yourself, and this use of scent is one of the more subtle aspects of gardening. To do so, you should arrange for the scented plants to 'arrive' at or approaching head height, or near to where you are likely to linger. To this end you might grow the smaller daphnes in raised beds, scented climbing roses on a pergola, *Viburnum carlesii* 'Aurora' near the garden frame, and nicotianas, mignonette and night-scented stocks around the part of the garden where you sit out on summer evenings.

It is a good idea to plant the general run of scented plants (all other aspects of your design being equal) towards the centre of the garden, rather than at the boundaries. You will then be able to enjoy them no matter in which direction the wind happens to be blowing.

IRIS PROTECTION
If heavy rain or snow threatens while Iris reticulata *is in flower, have a pane of glass ready with which to protect the blooms. They are very tough, but can look tatty after a battering.*

LILIES IN POTS
If you receive lily bulbs now, plant them in pots, plunge them in a cold frame, and plant out the entire pot contents in two months' time, cushioning the bottoms of the planting holes with 3cm (1¼in) of sand.

FEBRUARY

23

plants
OF THE
month

HELLEBORE
Helleborus orientalis

Depending on your botanical viewpoint, the Lenten rose is either a very variable species or one of about five. As gardeners rarely involve themselves in botany if they have any sense, they may take it that we are talking about those beautiful hellebores that flower in late winter and early spring and have nodding flowers in shades of purple and plum, usually beautifully spotted inside, and occasionally almost white, with some of the darkest approaching black.

type	Evergreen perennial
flowers	Wide open, nodding, saucer shaped
foliage	Dark green. The leaves lie flat, allowing the flowering stems to rise unobstructed
height	45cm (18in)
spread	60cm (2ft)
hardiness	Hardy
planting	Preferably in spring, but autumn planting is satisfactory for pot-grown plants
position	Part shade
soil	A good, organic, moisture-retentive soil
propagation	By division of established clumps only, immediately after flowering. Seeds should be sown as soon as ripe
varieties	There are many and they should be chosen if possible when in flower. The species you may find them under are *H. guttatus, olympicus* and *abschasicus*

CAMELLIA
Camellia × *williamsii* 'St Ewe'

Camellias as a whole have a long season that varies greatly according to the climate. In the south-eastern states of the USA, for example, flowering is well under way in autumn and is over by the end of this month. In the British Isles the first williamsii camellias are out this month in the south, and start a season that finishes with the last japonicas towards the end of spring. The further north you go, the later the camellia seasons get, but they are also more compressed, so that camellias flowers are rarely seen after mid-spring.

type	Evergreen shrub (*C. japonica* × C. *saluenensis*)
flowers	Funnel shaped, single, deep phlox-pink
foliage	Semi-glossy, pointed
height	1.5m (5ft) after 10 years
spread	1.2m (4ft) after 10 years
hardiness	One of the hardier camellias, but requiring shelter from freezing winds, particularly when young
position	Part shade. Camellias should never face the morning sun as frozen buds are killed if they thaw too quickly. In cooler areas, camellias should face south but have a little shade from the hottest sun at midday. Here, the williamsii camellias flower very much better than the varieties of *C. japonica*
soil	Lime-free, leafy, moisture-retentive but well-drained soil
pruning	None
propagation	By semi-ripe cuttings taken after midsummer and rooted under mist
alternatives	Many. Among the most celebrated williamsii camellias are 'Donation', large, semi-double, pink; 'Anticipation', medium, deep rose, peony-form double; 'Brigadoon', medium to large, semi-double, wavy, pink; and 'Debbie', neon-pink, large, ruffled peony-form double

CAMELLIA × WILLIAMSII 'ST EWE'

GARRYA ELLIPTICA

PRUNUS
Prunus mume 'Beni-Chidore'

This form of the Japanese apricot demonstrates the flexibility of trees and shrubs that flower as winter gives way to spring. It will, in a mild or even reasonable year, cover itself with blossom even in midwinter, while in harder years it may wait until well into spring. It is sensational when flowering with *hamamelis*, particularly those with clear yellow flowers, and it is worth planting for the association even though their flowering may not always coincide.

type	Small deciduous tree
flowers	Rich, dark phlox-pink, single (not double as sometimes stated) almond-scented, up to 9mm (¼in) wide
foliage	Leaves up to 10cm (4in) long; long-pointed
height	3m (10ft) after 10 years
spread	3m (10ft) after 10 years
hardiness	Hardy
position	Sun or part shade, sheltered
soil	Any good garden soil
pruning	None
propagation	Hardwood cuttings taken in autumn may root
special comment	Although the name given above is the one I believe to be correct, you may find it as 'Ben-shidon', 'Beni-shidare', or 'Beni-shidori'

GARRYA
Garrya elliptica

In places where the winters are mild, this unusual and strangely beautiful evergreen shrub thrives and produces its large crops of silvery-grey catkins at some time during mid- to late winter. If sheltered from winds it will tolerate quite severe cold, but it is not safe in the colder regions.

type	Evergreen shrub
flowers	Catkins like silky tassels. They are longer in male forms, which are the ones usually sold. Their average length is 15cm (6in) in colder areas, 25–30cm (10–12in) in warm ones
foliage	Leaves tough, leathery, roundish, dark glossy green above and woolly-grey beneath
height	Dependent on climate; 1.8–3.5m (6–12ft) after 10 years
spread	Dependent on climate; 1–2m (3–7ft) after 10 years
hardiness	See above
position	Part shade, shelter
soil	Any reasonable garden soil
pruning	None
propagation	By semi-ripe cuttings taken in summer and rooted under mist. In early autumn they may be tried in a garden frame
varieties	*G.e.* 'James Roof', if the true plant can be obtained, has catkins well over 30cm (1ft) long

tasks

FOR THE

month

2

PROPAGATION

SOWING SEED

This is the best time for sowing seed of trees and shrubs. I also sow many perennials now, under the same conditions, as I prefer to give them the longest growing season possible in their first year.

Early sowing is best done with some artificial heat. I use a frame on the greenhouse bench, which is fitted with under-soil heating cables, but for small quantities of seed heated propagators are perfectly adequate. Soilless compost seems to give far higher germination rates than a soil-based, John Innes type of compost.

Seed sowing can become far too complicated. The majority of these sorts of plants can be given identical treatment as far as compost, watering and the germination environment go. If you have no artificial heat, simply sow everything in pots in a cold frame. Different seeds will come up in different environments. With artificial heat, plants from warmer countries will germinate readily; in a cold frame, it will be cold-country plants that emerge in the main.

Far more important than technical details is an understanding of what makes seeds germinate, and what can inhibit them.

Factors in germination
The germination of seeds is governed by moisture, temperature and light. They act like alarms, waking the seed from its sleep. All three have to act in the right way, otherwise the seed will not awaken and start the chemical processes that lead to germination. Moisture must enter the seed and

must be constant or nearly so in the environment of the seed. The temperature must be at the right level and constant within certain limits. The amount of light falling on the seed must be within certain limits.

WARNING

■ *Inconsistency is death to most seeds. Fluctuating moisture, a failure of the temperature to 'inform' the seed that it is safe to germinate, and too much or too little light will severely inhibit germination* ■

You should water the seeds regularly but not heavily. You should keep the temperature within a fairly constant range, and you should provide about 50 per cent of the ambient light by shading the frame or propagator, but not too heavily. Light is also governed by the depth of soil over the seed. Cover the seeds with a depth of compost no deeper than the breadth of the seed. The smallest seeds – primulas, meconopsis, hydrangeas and so on, as well as certain other specific seeds, such as birches – should not be covered at all.

Seed dormancy
A fairly constant temperature of about 18°C (64°F) will 'convince' most seeds that spring has arrived and that it is safe to germinate. Other seeds, however, are more sceptical and need more evidence than that. They have to go through a notion of winter first, otherwise their inhibition mechanisms will not be broken down. Still others, less sophisticated, have time-delay mechanisms in the

shape of hard, impenetrable seed coats.

To deal with the former kinds, two methods are open. One is to sow all seeds from cold countries in a frame in autumn and let the fluctuating temperatures of winter do their job. However, not all such seeds are available to you in autumn. You can still sow them in a frame if they arrive in the early part of the year. Some will receive enough information, while those that do not will wait another year or even two. Thus, a gardener with no more than an unheated frame and some patience will obtain good results, but in the longer term.

The second method is to break the dormancy by 'kidding' the seed that winter has been and gone and that spring has arrived. Many cold-country seeds, including a large number of alpines, appreciate being mixed with a mixture of damp sand and peat in plastic bags and placed in the refrigerator for thirty days or so. They can then be removed for a few hours to warm up and then given another ten days, after which the entire mixture can be sown in heat. Or, you can sow the seed, wrap each pot in clingfilm, and put it in the fridge. It is a mistake to think of seed as being frozen; 'chilled' describes it much better.

The second kind of dormancy, that engendered by tough seed coats or those with built-in chemical inhibitors, has to be broken down mechanically. The pea family is notorious for this. Sowing in autumn in a frame allows hard coats to be rotted away naturally and chemical inhibitors to be leached out. Spring or late-winter seed may be soaked in water that starts hand hot and is then allowed to stand for 24 hours, after which the seeds are sown normally.

plants
IN
flower

TREES

TREES	colour	flower type
Prunus mume vars	Red, pink or white	Various
***Rhododendron arboreum** forms and hybrids	Red, pink or white	Trusses

SHRUBS

SHRUBS		
Abeliophyllum distichum	White, tinged pink	Small, fragrant
***Camellia × williamsii** vars (a few)	Various	Various
Cornus mas vars	Yellow	Small, on bare twigs
Daphne mezereum	Pink	On bare branches, fragrant
odora *'Aureomarginata'	Purplish	Fragrant
***Mahonia japonica**	Yellow	Drooping racemes, fragrant
***Rhododendron dauricum**	Rose-purple	Funnel shaped
*'Praecox' group	Rose-purple	Funnel shaped

Also: **Camellia sasanqua** vars, **Chimonanthus praecox**, **Erica carnea** vars, **E. × darleyensis** vars, **Garrya elliptica**, **Hamamelis**, **Jasminum nudiflorum**, **Lonicera fragrantissima**, **L. × purpusii**, **L. standishii**, **Sarcococca**, **Viburnum × bodnantense** vars, **V. farreri**.

CLIMBERS

CLIMBERS		
***Clematis cirrhosa balearica** (Fern-leaved clematis)	Pale yellow, red spots	

PERENNIALS

PERENNIALS	colour	height
***Bergenia** vars	White, pink or red	30cm (12in)
Helleborus orientalis vars	Plum, purple or white	60cm (24in)
***Iris unguicularis** and vars		

BULBS

BULBS	colour	height
Crocus chrysanthus vars	Yellow, blue, purple, white	8cm (3in)
angustifolius	Yellow and bronze	8cm (3in)
biflorus and vars	White or grey-white	9cm (3½in)
sieberi vars	White, blue or violet	8cm (3in)
Galanthus (Snowdrop) many	White, green markings	10cm (4in) average
Iris reticulata vars	Blue, reddish purple	15cm (6in)
Narcissus asturiensis	Golden yellow	20cm (8in)
bulbocodium vars	Yellow, hooped petticoats	15cm (6in)
'February Gold'	Yellow	30cm (12in)
'February Silver'	White, lemon cup	30cm (12in)
'Peeping Tom'	Yellow, reflexed	40cm (16in)

Also: A few other narcissus vars, **Eranthis hyemalis**, **Iris histriodes major**, **Cyclamen coum** aggregate

KEY

* = evergreen   spp = species
vars = varieties

NOTES

Rhododendrons prefer lime-free soil as do **camellias.**

ROCK GARDEN

Hepatica spp
***Polygala chamaebuxus**
Primula marginata
***Saxifraga** (**kabschia** and **engleria** spp and vars)
Also the smaller bulbs

MARCH

In our hearts those of us who know anything worth
knowing know that in March a new year begins . . .

JOSEPH WOOD KRUTCH
The Twelve Seasons (1949)

*Spring comes in several different ways for the gardener. There is
the official season, of course, the one that starts with the equinox;
but for most of us who watch plants grow, spring has been under
way for some time by then.*

*Did it start when the snowdrops hopefully declared the hostilities
of winter to be over? Some people, invariably optimistic by
nature, would say that the true spring began even earlier, with the
first lengthening of the days, when* Iris danfordiae *joined the most
precocious crocuses in braving the ferocity of those last winter
days. In fact the coming of spring varies by several weeks from one
area to another. If we are to be scientific about it, and I suppose
we should, the best criterion is based on the average soil
temperature above which plant growth can take place –*
5°C (41°F).

*What gardeners everywhere have in common is a capacity for
simply feeling the arrival of spring. It is not an occasion that is
marked off on the calendar like an annual holiday, nor is the
secret of its magic to be found in the bulb of a thermometer. It is a
stirring in the soul, a bubbling up of the spirit. Spring renders you
impatient of wintry pastimes and draws you gently but inexorably
outside. It is at this moment that the gardening year really begins.
The long largo of the overture ends as the allegro vivace of spring
moves into brisk, happy brilliance. For the great majority of us,
it is happening now.*

tasks

FOR THE

month

1

SETTLE BACK
Look for newly planted perennials and any alpines that have been lifted by frost and settle them back in the soil, firming finally with the foot where possible.

CHECKLIST

- ☐ Carry out path cleaning and maintenance
- ☐ Treat bearded irises against fungi
- ☐ Start dealing with slugs
- ☐ Prune roses, hydrangeas and buddleias
- ☐ Get your main planting season under way

MAINTENANCE

PATHS

Algae are highly dangerous on paths so it is worth a little labour to get rid of them. By the early spring every path laid with 'pavers', slabs, stone, or any material without a really rough finish will have developed by the early spring a coating of invisible algae as frictionless as a skating rink.

Obtain some potassium permanganate, also known as permanganate of potash, from your pharmacist. It comes as purple crystals and a few grams cost very little. Dissolve some in your watering can until the solution is about the colour of Beaujolais nouveau. If you don't know what it is like, imagine the colour of the phoniest wine you can think of, and that will be it. Water the path and leave it for 24 hours. Then take your yard brush, sluice the path down with clean water and scrub,

WARNING

- *Go carefully over any paving you have. Frost can lift this, and in an increasingly litigious society it might cost you a lot of money if a tradesman or visitor should trip* ■

wetting whenever you need to. The original colour of the path, dulled by algae and general dirt, will be restored, and, when it dries, the path will hold a wet wellington boot in full flight.

Apply a residual contact and pre-emergent weed-killer to gravel drives and paths. Applied this month it will give a year's protection against weeds; if you wait until later it may be too late, as it does not work well once the soil warms up.

IRIS RENOVATION

Bearded irises are all the better for being treated to a little surgery. Lift them – it is easy because their rhizomes are on the surface – and cut away any parts of rhizome that are diseased, squashy or extremely elderly. Cut with a very sharp, extremely clean knife, and dust the cuts with flowers of sulphur. Remove all dead leaves from the rhizomes and surrounding soil and put down bait for slugs.

When replanting them, scatter a few generous handfuls of bonemeal over their patch. It will feed the irises slowly and will also help to keep the soil on the alkaline side, which they like. If your soil is acid, it does no harm to add a handful of hydrated lime, too. However, you must not add lime if you are also giving the irises any animal manure. The lime reacts with the nitrates in the manure to give off ammonia, and all the goodness is lost.

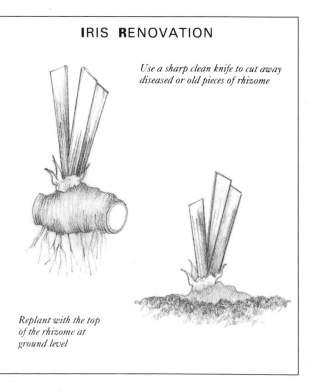

IRIS RENOVATION

Use a sharp clean knife to cut away diseased or old pieces of rhizome

Replant with the top of the rhizome at ground level

SLUG BAITING

Slugs mainly take bait at night. The bait is harmful to birds, which may come across doped, dehydrated, but still living slugs in the morning. If they eat them, they probably eat undigested bait as well. However, you have to fight slugs if you want a good garden, so rise early and pick the offending objects up. Gardens with plenty of birds have few slug problems, so think twice before accepting a kitten. It will grow up to be a highly efficient bird-scarer.

NOTE

▪ Go over the garden with a critical eye for dead leaves, heaps of blown twigs and general litter. Woodlice, slugs, snails, vine weevils and other animal pests love to hide and breed among such rubbish, and disease fungi thrive ▪

PRUNING HYDRANGEAS

Now is the best time for pruning hydrangeas and removing any dead heads left on to protect the buds underneath from frost. Cut back strong shoots to the first pair of fat buds (they are opposite one another). Next, go down to ground level and remove old, weak and crossing branches at the bottoms of the bushes. This will induce thick, hearty new shoots to arise from near the ground.

Annual pruning of *Hydrangea paniculata*, by cutting back each of last year's flowering stems to within a few centimetres of the old wood, is not recommended. The result looks like a horticultural cripple. Pruning like this is essential once in a while, otherwise flowering falls off, but every three years is quite enough.

PRUNING BUDDLEIA

Varieties of common buddleia should be pruned now, too. It is astonishing how drastic you can be with them. Nothing looks worse than a spindly buddleia, and the way to produce a vigorous, well-furnished shrub is to cut it down to within 45cm (18in) of the ground – every year. Buddleias seem to live on thin air, and I have carried out this treatment on specimens growing in nothing but old rubble for years and years. Every summer, without fail, there are the butterflies having a whale of a time on the massed flowerheads of the healthiest buddleias for miles around.

Yellow buddleias are different. *B. globosa* should be pruned seldom if at all, and its hybrid, *B.* x *weyerana*, of which there are some lovely forms without any mauve in the yellow, will need hardish pruning about once every six or seven years.

PRUNING ROSES

Prune the roses. Would that it were that simple! However, it does not have to be the solemn ritual that many would have you believe. Hybrid Teas and floribundas need quite hard pruning. This is because they produce their flowers on new wood and you want to induce a lot of it. The harder you prune at this time of year, the greater the response. Light pruning creates a twiggy mass of shoots and many flowers, but these will be on the small side; prune hard and you induce fewer but longer and stouter shoots, and fewer but larger flowers because the shoot buds left on the old wood will be fewer. Also aim

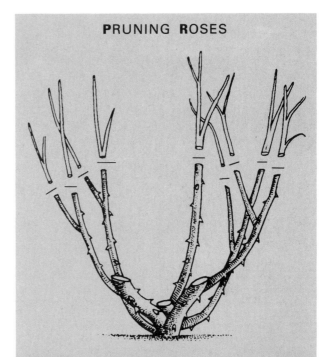

PRUNING ROSES

▪ With both hybrid teas and floribundas, cut out dead and diseased wood, pruning back any damaged shoots to good wood. Remove weak or crossing shoots then cut everything to between 15 and 22cm (6–9in) from the ground ▪

to remove crossing branches and encourage an open, chalice-shaped bush. This is where the 'prune to an outward-facing bud' advice comes in. Although not cast in tablets of stone, it is common sense.

PLANTS FROM POTS

Planting of shrubs, trees and perennials from pots can start as soon as the weather feels spring-like and the soil less like a cold, wet sponge.

BARE-ROOTED PLANTS

Anything arriving bare-rooted should be put in as soon as ever it is possible, as this is about its last chance. Plant them to the depth mark left from when they were in nursery containers.

FEEDING ALPINES
Top dress alpines with hoof and horn for slow-release nitrogen, and top up the surface layer of pebbles to about 2.5cm (1in) deep.

plants
OF THE
month

PLANTING TIMES
Please note that, as almost all trees and shrubs are sold in containers, they can be planted at any time of the year unless the ground is waterlogged or frozen. In this book, planting times are only given for perennials, which may be supplied bare-rooted, and for bulbs.

FORSYTHIA
Forsythia – 'Beatrix Ferrand'

Forsythias are among the most colourful of the shrubs that flower in early spring, with bright yellow blooms on the naked branches. They are hardy, reliable and, especially when a good variety is chosen, very free flowering. The flowers of *F.* 'Beatrix Ferrand' are particularly large.

type	Deciduous shrub
flowers	Rich canary yellow
foliage	Leaves 10cm (4in) long, slender, and fresh green
height	2m (7ft) after 10 years
spread	1m (40in) after 10 years
hardiness	Hardy
position	Full sun or part shade
soil	Any good garden soil
pruning	Immediately after flowering, cut back old flowering shoots to within 5cm (2in) of the old wood and remove crowded or crossing branches. Forsythia hedges should be trimmed hard after flowering
propagation	By semi-ripe cuttings, early to mid-summer. Root in a propagator at 15.5°C (60°F). Hardwood

cuttings taken in late autumn will root in a cold frame

alternatives	'Karl Sax' is similar in colour and has leaves that turn purple in autumn. *F. viridissima* 'Bronxensis' is a dwarf form for small gardens and is later flowering

HELLEBORE
Helleborus corsicus

In an unconventional way, this is one of the most beautiful of all garden plants, let alone those that flower in winter and early spring. It usually flowers now although it may be earlier. It is easy to grow.

type	Evergreen perennial
flowers	Drooping, pale green cups
foliage	Leaves have three prickly-edged, grey-green leaflets
height	60cm (2ft)
spread	90cm (3ft)
hardiness	Hardy, but should be protected from freezing winds
planting	Usually container-grown; plant any time in open weather
position	Sun or part shade, sheltered from cold winds

MAGNOLIA CAMPBELLII VAR. MOLLICOMATA

soil | Any good garden soil
propagation | Divide the plants immediately after flowering and plant straight away. Sow seeds in late spring in an outdoor seed bed

MAGNOLIA

Magnolia campbellii var. *mollicomata*

This is hardier than the larger *M. campbellii*. It flowers later in the season and is not as likely to lose its flowers to frosts. This variety also flowers at about twelve years old instead of thirty or more.

type | Tree
flowers | Very large, like pink waterlilies, before the leaves
foliage | Large and paddle shaped
height | 3m (10ft) after 10 years
spread | 2.5m (8ft) after 10 years
hardiness | The tree itself is reasonably hardy. Flowers are spoiled by hard frosts, but shelter helps to protect them
position | Part shade, protected from frosty winds
soil | Peaty or leafy, lime-free soil. Add well-rotted organic matter generously when planting
pruning | None
propagation | From seed, sown as soon as ripe

SCILLA

Scilla sibirica

There are several species and varieties of scilla. These are underrated plants, ideal for the rock garden and places such as occur round the boles of mature trees or among the trunks of smaller ones. They are most attractive when grown among patches of early daffodils.

types | Bulbs
flowers | Star shaped, shades of blue and violet-blue
height | 5-10cm (2-4in)
spread | Clump-forming
hardiness | Hardy
planting | Plant 8cm (3in) apart and 8cm (3in) deep in early autumn
position | Partial shade and in company with other small bulbs
soil | Any good garden soil
propagation | Divide the clumps, which increase freely, in summer when dormant, or in leaf immediately after flowering

FORSYTHIA 'BEATRIX FERRAND'

alternatives | Try to obtain the variety 'Spring Beauty', which is deeper blue. *S. tubergeniana* is earlier-flowering as is *S. bifolia*, which has a longer flowering period. All have blue flowers

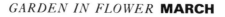
tasks
FOR THE
month
2

NOTE

Hemerocallis prefer not to be disturbed more than once in every five or six years. They should be left alone until flowering declines perceptibly

CHECKLIST

☐ Divide perennials of all kinds
☐ Plan bulb planting carefully

PROPAGATION

DIVIDING PERENNIALS

This is quite the best time for dividing perennials of all kinds. The soil is – well, we hope it is – warming up, and the plants are at a stage when they are bursting with urgency, positively longing to put out new roots and get on with growing.

Primulas

Primulas enjoy being divided, and it is a satisfying task. Lift a good clump and soak off the soil in a bucket of water. Ease the soil right away and the plant begins to fall apart into individual crowns. A little gentle teasing and tugging soon leaves plenty of young plants – and some for your neighbour, too.

Gentians

If you have the good fortune to grow Asiatic gentians – the kind that flower from late summer onwards on lime-free, peaty soils – divide them now.

At the moment, the growing plants show as buttons of green, just extending into individual stems. These are at the heads of stout, white, thong-like roots. Often there will be more than one crown per button, and they tease apart with the greatest of ease if you are deft. Plant them immediately, allowing about a hand's-span between them, and autumn should bring a dazzling show of sumptuous blue.

Achilleas and larger herbaceous perennials

Larger herbaceous perennials can be lifted and attacked with unplantsmanlike ferocity. The roots of an old clump of achillea are like so much fine wire and about as penetrable. Take two garden forks and thrust them back to back into the clump. Done properly, this leaves the handles at an outward angle to one another. Press the handles together and immediately wrench them apart. The achillea should split into two with a crack.

Of course you may find yourself indulging in a wrestling match with your plant. Little harm will be done, and you can go on subdividing until you have several small, wholesome divisions, each furnished with a few strong young crowns and a plentiful share of roots. Make sure the roots are actually attached to the crowns. Throw away the tired centre of the old plant.

PLANNING

BULBS

Lack of planning is one of the main reasons why bulbs are often not used as well as they could be in private gardens. Trained gardeners and bulb experts can do the most wonderful things with bulbs, chiefly because they plan ahead, but most people lead busy lives doing other things, and planning is easier said than done.

Unlike other plants, bulbs are not easily bought on impulse, unless you are taken in by the pictures that usually accompany the bins of bulbs on sale in autumn. A particular daffodil seen in flower in spring cannot be

DIVIDING PRIMULAS

bought straight away; you have to wait for six months, by which time it is highly likely that you will have forgotten all about it.

Use the spring to gather information. There is no substitute for seeing bulbs in growth, and visits to gardens that are open to the public can be supplemented by keeping your eyes and mind open to them in other people's private gardens as you pass by.

Public gardens have the advantage of labels, and it is a mistake to visit one without a notebook. Write down the name of the bulb and a short description of it. If, subsequently, that variety is not available, this description will be helpful in choosing something else close enough to give much the same effect. I once made a note to, 'Remember *Narcissus* 'Ice Wings; new white cyclamineus hybrid, approx 10in'. It was growing in the famous Keukenhof garden in Holland and had pure white flowers and neatly swept-back petals. That autumn, I could not find 'Ice Wings' on sale anywhere, so bought a few bulbs of 'Dove Wings' instead. 'Wings' in the name of each variety refers to the characteristically backswept petals of this group of hybrids. 'Dove Wings' differs from 'Ice Wings' in that it has a pale yellow trumpet with its white petals and is a couple of inches taller. The main thing was that it was quite easily obtainable and would fit my planting scheme almost as well.

NOTE

■ *After flowering allow the leaves of bulbs to die down, thus replenishing the bulb for next year's display* ■

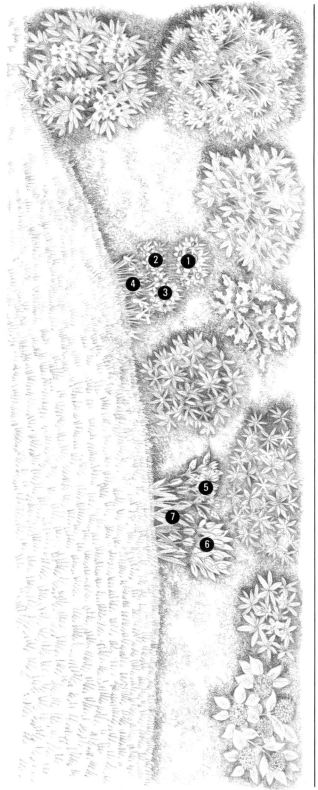

KEY

1 ***Narcissus* 'Suzy'**
2 ***N.* 'Scarlet Gem'**
3 ***N.* 'Actaea'**
4 ***N.* 'Tête à Tête'**
5 ***Tulipa* 'Juan'**
6 ***T.* 'Candela'**
7 ***T.* 'Berlioz'**

MAPPING OUT YOUR DISPLAY
Draw a 'map' of your border (see below) – or wherever you will be planting bulbs in the autumn – and designate areas for where you would like bulbs. Then look at those in flower and choose the bulbs that, ideally, you would like. If a particular niche cannot be filled, write 'red, short-stemmed tulip' or whatever, and see what is on offer when the time comes. How it should turn out is shown left.

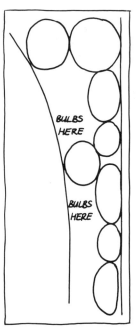

BULBS HERE

BULBS HERE

plant
selections

PERENNIALS

The great majority of perennials are easy to divide. However, a few are best propagated by other methods and you should not try to divide them:

Althaea
Anemone (some)
Aquilegia
Codonopsis
Cynoglossum
Dianthus
Erodium
Euphorbia myrsinites
Gentiana (except autumn-flowering gentians)
Gypsophila
Helleborus
Incarvillea
Linum
Lysichitum
Malva
Ostrowskia
Phlox (border)
Phyteuma
Platycodon
Primula denticulata
Salvia (some)
Verbascum

PERENNIALS

Pulmonarias are among the most valuable groundcover plants you can grow. Choose a selection of species for flowers throughout spring. Their foliage, evergreen with the exception of *P. angustifolia*, is always present, lending an intriguing note in its often silvery-spotted dress. Pulmonarias are happy to spread gently in light shade, and the bright pink flowers of *P. officinalis* have a tone that is strong enough to cope with early spring light. This species was grown in gardens for medicinal use. It was known as Lungwort, since the Doctrine of Signatures decreed that because a diseased lung lobe was blotched and spotted, the leaves, also spotted and much the same shape, must contain the cure. We shouldn't scoff: many gardening practices are based on even flimsier premises.

BULBS

Spring and **daffodils** are inseparable, and they are now well into their stride. The choice is extremely wide and often daunting, with the catalogues bright with pictures of tall, gracious 'daffs' and long-stemmed, elegant 'narcissi'. There are few sights as magical as a daffodil-strewn wood or glade; if you have the room, plant as many of these cool beauties as you possibly can.

The great majority of gardens, however, are quite small, and large flowers on stems of 45cm (18in) or more seem out of scale and tend to be planted in blobby clumps because drifts of them become overpowering. This is where the dwarf and shorter-stemmed daffodils are so valuable; not just because they are in scale, but also because the owner of an average garden can enjoy so many more varieties.

PULMONARIA OFFICINALIS

Narcissus 'Tête à Tête' is only 15cm (6in) high but holds its twin heads up in the teeth of the most bellicose gales. Almost every stem has two flowers, perfect miniature daffodils in bright golden yellow. The Lent lily, *Narcissus pseudonarcissus*, one form of which is the Tenby daffodil, differs from the wild daffodils to be seen elsewhere in Britain in that its petals are the same deep yellow as the trumpet; those that Wordsworth saw had light yellow, contrasting petals. It only grows 15–30cm (6–12in) high so if you have room, naturalise it in grass, but if not, it is still small enough to provide a host of daffodils even more golden than those that so entranced him. *Narcissus cyclamineus* 'Jumblie' has the swept-back petals of the species combined with the simple grace of the true daffodil. 'Little Witch', obviously a kissing cousin of 'Jumblie' and well under 30cm (1ft) high, carries on flowering into later spring.

Chionodoxas are close relatives of the starry-flowered, blue scillas. The most widely grown is *Chionodoxa luciliae*, often known as 'glory of the snow', although it is said that the name refers to its flowering as the snows melt in the mountains of Turkey. It is only 13cm (5in) in height and makes a charming clump of starry flowers of an eye-catching, vivid blue. *C. sardensis*, which is about the same height, is as brilliant a gentian blue as you could wish to see twinkling at you on a bare day.

The big, fat 'Dutch' **crocuses** flower this month, and they are preferred by many gardeners for their size. They lack the natural air that seems so essential in flowers if they are to carry off such an early appearance, and they can appear coarse. Nevertheless, they have their place and are ebulliently cheerful.

●

SHRUBS

Rhododendron 'Praecox', is among the earliest of all shrubs. Generally speaking, early-flowering rhododendrons cause as many heartbreaks as a bevy of debutantes. A whiff of frost – no rare occurrence this month – and the flowers are gone for another year, crumpled brown mush at the branch ends. 'Praecox' is made of sterner stuff and, as long as it is in shelter, will survive to continue its display of rosy purple.

Stachyurus praecox is a shrub whose 10cm (4in) flower-tassels are formed in autumn to open unerringly in spring. They hang stiffly down, not a leaf in sight, with up to twenty-four small golden cups ranged along them. It belongs in more spacious gardens not because it is very large, but because its appeal is limited

MAHONIA AQUIFOLIUM

to its budding and flowering. For more prolonged interest, there is 'Magpie', a variety of *S. chinensis*, which flowers two weeks later. Its leaves have white margins with a pink blush – most effective in a shady spot.

Mahonias bear long tassels of gold too. These may be upright or lax or – as in *Mahonia aquifolium* – what the botanists call 'terminal clusters'. This species is, according to our chronology, the earliest, as its more distinguished congeners flower mainly in winter, which for us is late, not early. It is a plant that combines humility with determination, and its holly-like, evergreen foliage is to be treasured, rather than scorned. Solicitude pays off – if it is allowed decent light it gives a bright show of bold, golden flowers set off against the occasional scarlet tint among its foliage.

No two components of a floral arrangement go better than fresh spring daffodils and **willow** catkins when they are at their velvety best.

Pussy-willows appear on the naked branches and have a way of catching the low, seasonal light that induces moments of magic of the kind that are the stuff of nostalgia. You may hanker for sub-tropical warmth as you listen to the lashing rain, but if you were eventually to move to warmer climes would you not occasionally pine for that pale sunlight, picking out the tinsel on the lowly willow flowers?

plants

IN

flower

KEY

* = evergreen   spp = species
vars = varieties

NOTES

Many **Prunus** have other points of interest, such as:

P. sargentii coloured bark
P. cerasifera 'Pissardii' purple leaves
P. 'Moerheimii is a weeping form
P. 'Pandora' has rich autumn colour.

HEATHER

Varieties of Erica carnea and E. × darleyensis are lime-tolerant.

TULIPS IN TUBS

Devote one or two containers to Kaufmanniana tulips. Set off their strongest colours, like the red of 'Show Winner' or the orange and salmon of 'Shakespeare', against the foliage of an evergreen shrub. *Pieris* 'Forest Flame' is a good companion for them, as it will turn red itself next month when its new foliage unfurls, and then carry on a spectacular foliage display into the beginnings of summer.

TREES	colour	flower type
Magnolia campbellii mollicomata	Purplish pink	V. large, open saucer-shaped
dawsoniana	Pale rose	Large, flat
denudata	White	Cup-shaped, fragrant
Prunus cerasifera 'Pissardii'	White from pink buds	Small, but profusely borne
dulcis (Almond)	White or pink	Single or double
incisa (Fuji cherry)	White, from pink buds	Small, freely borne
'Kursar'	Deep pink	Small, freely borne
'Moerheimii'	White, pink in bud	Small, freely borne
mume (Japanese apricot)	Pink to almost red	Single to semi-double
'Okame'	Carmine	Small freely borne
'Pandora'	Pale pink	
sargentii	Pink	Single
subhirtella	Pink	Small
× yedoensis	White, blushed	Single, almond scented
*Rhododendron arboreum and hybrids (mild areas only)	White, pink or red	Trusses
Salix aegyptica	Yellow	Catkins
SHRUBS		
Camellia japonica vars	Various	Various
Chaenomeles speciosa vars	White to crimson	Small saucers
Corylopsis pauciflora	Yellow	Short racemes, scented
Daphne mezereum	Reddish purple	Scented
*Erica carnea vars	Various	
× darleyensis vars	Various	
Forsythia	Yellow	
Magnolia stellata	White	Star-shaped
*Mahonia aquifolium	Yellow	Close clusters
Rhododendron several, including **dauricum, leucaspis, oreodoxa** var. **fargesii, pemakoense, 'Praecox', racemosum, strigillosum, 'Seta'**		
Salix apoda	Catkins are silvery-furry, then become covered with yellow anthers	
caprea (Pussy willow)	Female form has silver catkins	
gracilistyla	Catkins are silvery grey at first, becoming red as pollen appears	
'Melanostachys'	Catkins almost black, becoming red, then yellow	

	colour	height
Stachyurus praecox	Yellow	Cup-shaped racemes of up to 24
chinensis	Yellow	Up to 35 flowers in a raceme
Viburnum tinus vars	White	Flattish heads

PERENNIALS

	colour	height
Helleborus corsicus	Green	60cm (2ft)
Primula farinosa	Lilac	15cm (6in)
rosea	Rose	15cm (6in)
denticulata	Various, red forms are most desirable	30cm (1ft)
Pulmonaria rubra	Coral red	30cm (1ft)
saccharata	Blue, from pink buds	30cm (1ft)
Saxifraga – cushion forms	Various	A few inches

BULBS

	colour	height
Anemone blanda	Various	10cm (4in)
Chionodoxa luciliae	Blue	13cm (5in)
'Pink Giant'	Pink	13cm (5in)
sardensis	Gentian blue	13cm (5in)
Crocus Dutch hybrids. Many others overlap from last month		
Muscari armenaicum	Cobalt blue	18cm (7in)
Narcissus – daffodil types and early 'narcissi' dwarfs, **'Apricot'**, **'Beryl'**, *cyclamineus*, **'Jumblie'**, **'Little Witch'**, **'Tête â tète'** and many more		
Scilla bifolia	Blue	4cm (10in)
sibirica **'Spring Beauty'**	Deep blue	20cm (8in)
Tulipa kaufmanniana hybrids	Various	13–20cm (5–8in)

ROCK GARDEN

	colour	height
Alyssum saxatile vars	Yellow	20–30cm (8–12in)
Aubrieta vars	Mauve, blue, purple	8–10cm (3–4in)
Draba sps	Yellow	5–10cm (2–4in)
Omphalodes verna	Bright blue	15cm (6in)
Primula denticulata	Pale lilac to deep red	30cm (1ft)
× *pubescens*	White, crimson, violet, brick red	7–12cm (2¾–8in)
Saxifraga oppositifolia	Red, purple, white	2cm (1in)

CONTAINER CONTRASTS

If you like gardening in tubs, urns, and other ornamental containers – or if your gardening is done in a city yard where you have no choice but to use them – you may find yourself with little colour in March. It is easy to brighten up your containers with small bulbs. Chionodoxas and scillas look lovely with very small daffodils, but be careful about tonal order. Choose a light-toned narcissus, such as the cyclamineus hybrid 'Ibis', which has reflexed, white petals and lemon-yellow trumpets on 20cm (8in) stems, and plant it with *Scilla sibirica* 'Spring Beauty', whose blue is deep and rich. Tonal order is the key to making grape hyacinth (*Muscari*) look right. They so often appear out of place because their blue, which is quite deep, often appears near yolk-yellow daffodils.

SILVER AND GREEN

In the open garden, you can set up a subtle, year-round foliage contrast by growing pulmonarias as ground cover beneath camellias. The slightly whiskery, matt, silver-dotted pulmonaria leaves highlight the glossy, deep green of the camellias, and they make a quietly splendid picture when flowering together.

HEATHER COMPANIONS

Erica carnea is a species that grows in limestone mountains – it is not a moorland heather. In nature, you find it associated with all sorts of other plants, many of them shrubby. Varieties of the species and of *E.* × *darleyensis* should be planted with suitable companions to give structure and purpose. Try small willows, which are perfect when placed among them. They can provide early colour where deciduous azaleas will bloom later, and the cool white of *E.* × *darleyensis* 'Silberschmelze' deceives nicely, hinting little at the hot oranges, reds and yellows that are to come.

APRIL

April, April,
Laugh thy girlish laughter;
Then, the moment after,
Weep thy girlish tears!

SIR WILLIAM WATSON
Collected Poems *(1905)*

This month is the early adolescence of the year; up one moment, down the next – never knowing when to smile or cry. Dawning poise and serenity are interrupted by stormy episodes when childhood seems to break through, but the promise is always there. Adulthood is just around the corner.

The weather is showery and cool, but the sun can be every bit as strong as it is in high summer. The soil is warming up quickly, absorbing heat faster than it is prepared to release it to warm the air. Plants whose natural home is the dappled shade of trees scamper into growth in the full light, in order to flower and set seed before the leaf canopy closes over.

This is pure spring; there is nothing transitional about it. This month rushes, bustles, agonises, has moments of forgetfulness, bursts into tears, and leaps with joyful life. It is a time when the patience of gardeners is sometimes sorely tried and when their ability to take the long view can be put to the test. Frosts are not as devastating as they can be a few weeks later, but it is a rare year when some flowers are not lost. On a well-drained slope this month is full of flower; in a frost pocket it is a lottery in which some years are almost completely barren of bloom.

There is still a wide difference between climatic zones. The full bubble and bounce of spring may not arrive for another month in colder, northern areas, and it is sometimes early summer before the seasons briefly coincide. Spring can be somewhat telescoped at higher latitudes and altitudes, but it is more a state of nature than a thirty-day period and always arrives – some time.

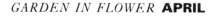

tasks

FOR THE

month

1

CHECKLIST

☐ Feed the lawn as necessary and begin regular mowing

☐ Mulch beds and borders

☐ Give roses a top dressing of fertiliser

☐ Stake herbaceous perennials

☐ Plant out any perennials raised from seed last summer

☐ Plant gladioli and dahlias

☐ Order alpines from specialist nurseries and plant out

☐ Prune *Kerria japonica*, forsythias and flowering currants when they have flowered

MAINTENANCE

THE LAWN

A flower garden with an unkempt lawn always looks shabby. Mowing is essential, but is also one of the most repetitive chores in gardening. There are, however, ways of reducing the frequency of the labour to give you more time for your plants.

The main one is to realise that almost everyone overfeeds their lawn. This is not only unnecessary but also produces soft, sappy, quick-growing grass that has to be mown often. Feed the lawn about one-third as often as most other people and you will have a good, hard-wearing lawn. Your mower will last much longer, and furthermore you will avoid adding to the excess of fertiliser that is leaching down to the water supplies and creating a major environmental problem. I feed my lawn once every *three years*.

Mark out a section of your lawn into square metres (yards) using bamboo canes. Apply the required amount of fertiliser and then move the canes on, until the complete lawn has been fed.

Mowing begins when the soil starts to lose its sogginess and the hardest frosts are over, which is usually this month. Unless you want to play bowls or practise your putting, there is no point in mowing with the blades set lower than 3cm (1¼in) – it only accelerates wear.

BEDS AND BORDERS

Make certain that all perennial weeds are absent and then, as the soil warms up, mulch with a weed-free material such as forest bark. This should preferably be 'composted' bark; if it is not, add 30g (1oz) of sulphate of ammonia per square metre (yard). This prevents the bark from taking nitrogen from the soil as it breaks down.

The mulch should be at least 4cm (1½in) deep to be effective. It will not only suppress weeds, but will also conserve moisture and make watering in summer much less of a necessity.

ROSES

Feed established roses with a rose fertiliser. Scatter 35g (1oz) over the root area of each rose and hoe in gently, taking care not to damage any main roots as this can stimulate suckering.

PERENNIALS

I prefer to support tall or floppy herbaceous perennials with twigs, much as one would peas. If you live in the town you may find them hard to obtain, and you will have to resort to bamboo and string or proprietary plant stakes.

Whichever supports you choose, have them ready at hand from now on and put them into place when the perennials break ground – if you leave it until early summer it will be too late.

If you cut twigs of willow, poplar or hazel, make sure to do so a couple of weeks before you need to use them or when they are put into the soil they will take root.

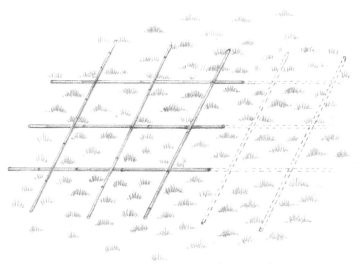

PLANTING

Dahlias

If you live away from the mild areas where dahlias can be grown in the ground all year, plant them out later in the month. Any new dahlia shoots could be frosted, so earth them up like potatoes.

Summer-flowering bulbs

Plant gladioli 10cm (4in) deep and ensure that the base of each corm is on soil and not over an air pocket. Well-rotted manure or garden compost can be dug in beforehand to provide good growing conditions. Peat is excellent on heavy soils, but only as a conditioner. Do not plant all your corms at once, but make successional plantings over a number of weeks in order to have a season of flowers, rather than one burst of bloom.

Early this month is your last chance for planting bulbs such as galtonias and especially lilies.

Alpines

In many areas this is the ideal month for planting alpines. It is also the time of year when alpine plant nurseries are getting into full swing with sending out their mail orders. The range of alpines that is sold in most garden centres is small, with often only the sketchiest descriptions to be found on the labels – and sometimes none at all. If you are a keen alpine grower it is better to order most of your plants by mail.

PRUNING

As soon as *Kerria japonica*, forsythias and flowering currants have finished flowering, prune them back to encourage them to produce flowering wood for next year. The best method is to remove some of the older stems at ground level and then clip back any others that are unwieldy or unbalancing the shrub.

BARE-ROOTED PLANTS
Beware of nurseries offering cheap, bare-rooted plants this month. You may think they are no end of a bargain, but they will fail. The time for open-ground plants is now well past.

WEED-FREE PLANTING
Whenever you plant a pot-grown specimen, always scoop away the top 0.5cm (¼in) or so of compost. This is where the weed seeds are, especially those of that awful pennycress which fires its seeds all over the place for months on end, germinates in what seems to be five minutes flat, and flowers again five minutes after that.

LABELS

Never plant anything without a label. You may think you can remember the names of the plants, but Murphy's Law decrees that you will forget just the one you thought you knew best.

Labels should be permanent, which is to say they should be legible after twenty years. By far the best are strips of anodised aluminium, on which ordinary pencil remains decipherable for more than two decades. Plastic of whatever kind looks ugly and succumbs to ultra-violet light in no time. So-called 'permanent' marking inks and many of the pens sold in garden centres for 'permanent, waterproof labelling' last about a year before they have you holding the labels up to the light as you vainly try to work out what on earth they used to say.

Form a 'stake' from 12 gauge wire as illustrated. Then bend an anodised aluminium label around the loop in the wire to make a permanent label.

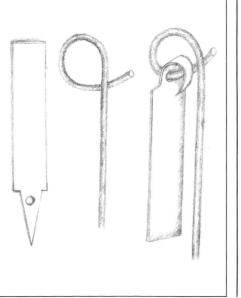

plants
OF THE
month

RHODODENDRON
Rhododendron Loderi

This name covers a group of hybrids between *R. fortunei* and *R. griffithianum*. They are considered to be the best hybrid rhododendrons ever raised and have very large, lily-like flowers in loose, many-flowered trusses. Their hardiness, free and regular flowering and delicious scent are inherited from *R. fortunei*.

type	Evergreen shrub
flowers	Vary, but usually some shade of pink, shading and fading more or less to cream or white
foliage	Leaves quite large and mid-green
height	2m (7ft) after 10 years
spread	2m (7ft) after 10 years
hardiness	These hybrids require shelter from wind. In shelter, they are hardy away from the coldest areas
position	Grow in the dappled shade of trees, preferably where you can enjoy their scent without getting wet and muddy. The larger the leaf of a rhododendron, the less sun it can take
soil	Must be lime free and as leafy as possible
pruning	None
propagation	Propagation of rhododendrons of this type is not easy and is best left to the nursery trade
varieties	All stand on their own merits
alternatives	*R. fortunei* bears bell-shaped, lilac-pink flowers next month; the subspecies *discolor*, which is strongly scented, bears its pale pink blooms in early to midsummer. There is no real alternative to *R.* Loderi in spring

AZALEA
Japanese Azaleas

The evergreen 'Japanese' azaleas are considerably shorter and more compact, and flower earlier, than the deciduous azaleas. These extremely well-known plants belong, in fact, to a special section of the genus *Rhododendron* and require the same conditions. However, they are also ideal for culture in raised beds or tubs, where a rhododendron-type soil can be used even in a limy garden.

type	Small, evergreen shrubs
flowers	A wide range of colours from white through various pinks and lilacs to red, including some doubles. In flower during second half of this month and first few days of next

RHODODENDRON LODERI

foliage	Leaves small and densely packed, making for neat, rounded bushes that are always decorative
height	0.5–1m (1½–3ft) after 10 years
spread	0.75–1.25m (2½–4ft) after 10 years
hardiness	Hardy, apart from a few of the older varieties, which are hardy only in milder areas
position	Plant in sun as long as the soil is moisture retentive, but try to allow for a little shade during the hottest part of the day
soil	Peaty, leafy and lime free
pruning	None
propagation	Take semi-ripe cuttings in summer and place in a heated propagator or mist unit. On no account attempt to pot up the rooted cuttings until they begin to grow again the following spring
varieties	All stand on their own merits

TRILLIUM GRANDIFLORUM

MAGNOLIA

Magnolia × soulangeana

This is the most familiar of all the magnolias, bearing its enormous chalices on bare branches in the best forms. There are several varieties, with flowers ranging from pure white to deep purple.

type	Tree or large shrub
flowers	White in 'Alba Superba' and 'Amabilis', variously shaded purple from the base, until fully red-purple in 'Rustica Rubra'
foliage	Large and paddle shaped
height	2m (7ft) after 10 years; 10m (35ft) after 30 years
spread	1.5m (5ft) after 10 years; 7m (24ft) after 30 years
hardiness	Hardy
position	Full sun or part shade
soil	The soil must be lime free. Add plenty of well-rotted organic matter to the soil. Magnolias dislike sticky clay. Dry, sandy soils should be thoroughly mixed with copious amounts of organic matter, but not fresh manure
pruning	None
propagation	By air layering in mid-spring or early summer. Simple layering is sometimes possible
alternatives	There are now many different kinds of this general type of magnolia. The following are excellent: 'Jane', 'Betty', 'Heaven Scent', *liliiflora* 'Nigra', 'Sayonara'

TRILLIUM

Trillium grandiflorum

Trilliums are among the aristocrats of spring flowers. They are often thought of as difficult, but if you follow the notes below you should find them no problem. All parts of the plant except the stems and roots are in threes – the leaves are in whorls of three, and the flowers have three petals.

type	Herbaceous perennial
flowers	White; there are single and double forms
foliage	Whorls of leaves at the tops of the stems, just below the flowers
height	30cm (1ft)
spread	30cm (1ft)
hardiness	Hardy
planting	Container-grown plants may be planted at any time in open weather. Plant open-ground specimens between mid-autumn and early spring
position	Part or complete shade, but not dry shade
soil	The peatier and leafier the soil the better. Trilliums abhor dryness, but must nevertheless have good drainage
propagation	By careful division in early autumn or early spring. Each division must have at least one growing point
alternatives	*T. sessile* and *T. chloropetalum* have flowers that vary from pink to deep maroon

tasks

FOR THE

month

2

CHECKLIST

- [ ] Check seed trays every day for signs of germination
- [ ] Prick out seedlings when large enough to handle
- [ ] Continue to sow hardy annuals in the positions in which they are to grow. Thin those that have germinated
- [ ] Continue dividing perennials
- [ ] Divide bulbs
- [ ] Pot up rooted cuttings
- [ ] Decide on container-grown or open-ground perennials

PROPAGATION

SEED

Examine pots and trays of seed every day. The purpose of this is so that you can take trays from the shade of a frame as soon as possible after germination and put the seedlings into full light so that they will remain short-stemmed and sturdy, and not become weak and drawn out.

Seeds that have been germinated over bottom heat, which includes most trees and shrubs, should be taken from their heated, humid environment and placed on the greenhouse bench in full light, but the temperature should not drop below 0°C (32°F).

Water freshly germinated seedlings with Cheshunt Compound in order to forestall damping-off disease. This should not be necessary, however, if you treated the trays at sowing time.

You should finish direct sowing of sweet peas now. Those you sowed in pots last month should be thoroughly hardened off and then planted out now.

If you sowed any hardy annuals last month, keep an eye on them. As soon as you can tell weed seedlings from plants, tweak them out while they are still small. Thin the plant seedlings at the same time, so as to produce short, bushy specimens. With a good, fertile soil you should not need to apply any fertiliser to them.

PRICKING OUT SEEDLINGS

Seedlings of trees, shrubs and perennials should be pricked out as soon as they can be handled. The conventional wisdom states that you should wait until there is a pair of true leaves in addition to the seed leaves (cotyledons). That is all very well, but many seedlings are far too small at that stage. The best advice is simply that you should prick seedlings out when they are large enough to handle – but of course when they have some true leaves.

The cotyledons of many seedlings make useful handles with which to hold them as they are lifted from the compost. On no account hold the stem of a seedling – it will be far too delicate to stand the lightest grip without becoming damaged. Lightly hold a cotyledon or leaf, and support the root ball underneath as you move the plant from the seed tray to its individual pot.

There are all sorts of gadgets for lifting seedlings. Most are designed to make twee little Christmas presents for gardening relatives. They are, by and large, useless and compare badly with the sensitivity and delicacy of which human fingers are capable.

PERENNIALS

Continue dividing perennials, but only those that flower late in summer. If you have not got round to those that flower earlier, such as oriental poppies, hemerocallis and iris, you should leave them until early autumn or early next spring, as they are now growing strongly and would be set back badly by being disturbed.

BULBS

It is not generally appreciated that many bulbs can be lifted and divided while still green. Just after flowering is the best time for daffodils and narcissi. I reserve this procedure for bulbs that are in the wrong place or that I have hitherto forgotten. Do not try to break down the clumps very far, look after the roots, and replant immediately. Remove the old flower stems so that the plant's energies do not go into making seed.

Bulbs are storage organs. They hold a reserve of food so that the plant is capable of a long resting period. The food is manufactured in the leaves so if they are removed or have knots tied in them this may result in the bulb not being formed properly and failing to flower in subsequent years.

The leaves should be left in place until they have turned quite yellow. Next month, as the danger of frosts recedes, you will be able to disguise them with plantings of annuals. Meanwhile leave them to get on with their job.

CUTTINGS

Many gardeners make the basic mistake of potting up all their cuttings soon after they have rooted. Many will tolerate it, and in fact it is the best thing to do with the majority, but there are some that bitterly resent it and they will die.

If you root your cuttings in pure sand you really have to pot them on quickly, but few of us do, and then usually only with soft cuttings (especially of alpines); the standard mixture – 50/50 by volume of moss peat and sand – will hold enough moisture to keep the plants going during the winter.

What kills the young plants is disturbance. No matter how careful you are you will still damage the root hairs, which are only one cell thick, and the plants are unable to renew them in the later part of the year. In spring, however, the plants are not attempting to go dormant but are growing fast, and the root hairs are quickly re-grown.

The plants most seriously affected are listed, although several more will succumb

to some degree. Potting of cuttings late in the year is a major cause of failure with magnolias and is also the reason for the extreme scarcity of the beautiful Chinese shrub *Dipelta floribunda,* which roots easily under a mist system but does not survive potting until the following spring.

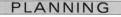

PLANNING

PERENNIALS

If you decide to carry out a planting project involving more than just a few perennials, it is a good idea to consider ordering open-ground plants for autumn delivery. They are larger and more robust than pot-grown plants and will give you a good display in their first year, whereas pot-grown perennials take two years to be effective. In the open ground, too, root growth is unrestricted, whereas perennials in pots rapidly become rootbound and very difficult to establish properly.

The decision whether to buy potted perennials or plants from the open ground should be taken now. If you decide to buy them in pots from the garden centre, make up your mind to visit about once every two weeks from next month onwards; otherwise, by the time you come to plant in autumn the best will have gone and you will be left with the rubbish. If, on the other hand, you choose bare-rooted, open-ground perennials, start your research now and determine to visit as many gardens open to the public as possible. The ideas for plants and plant associations that you pick up on these visits will make all the difference in the world to your ultimate design.

PERENNIALS TO DIVIDE

Aster
Helenium
Helianthus
Kniphofia
Monarda
Phlox
Rudbeckia

CUTTINGS TO POT UP IN SPRING

All these are prone to failure if potted up in autumn.

Azalea
Camellia
Conifers
Crinodendron
Cytisus (broom)
Eucryphia
Ilex (holly)
Rhododendron (many)

plant
selections

*Kaufmanniana
tulip 'Glück'*

BULBS

The difference between **'daffodils'** and **'narcissi'** is, of course, an artificial one. There are official groupings within the genus *Narcissus* that differentiate between 'Trumpet daffodils or narcissi of garden origin', and 'Large-cupped' and 'Small-cupped' narcissi of garden origin.

As far as I am concerned, a daffodil is what looks like a daffodil, and a narcissus is one of the sophisticated sorts of flowers that generally has a shorter cup, which is more openly flared and less trumpet-like. What matters is the fact that the flowers of 'narcissi' look more appropriate this month than earlier in the year.

Many modern narcissi are long-lasting in flower, and these are the ones that everyone with a garden that is on the small side should seek out. Plant just a few in fair-sized groups and you will obtain a much better effect than by trying to buy all the toys in the shop.

With the striking contrasts in modern narcissi between the colours of the petals and the cups, you can make for much stronger statements than were made by the innocent daffodils of last month. 'Professor Einstein', for example, which flowers early this month, has brilliant orange-red cups against pure white petals. 'Romance', which is later, is on the same plan but with smaller, lighter-coloured cups and is very long lasting. 'Actaea', which blooms late in the month, is beautifully scented. Its flowers have small cups, which are yellow with red rims, and broad, white petals.

Collectively, **tulips** have a far longer season than most gardeners realise. It starts in early spring, or sometimes even in late winter, when the dwarf Kaufmanniana hybrids trustingly open their wide, star-shaped flowers to the fickle weather, but begins in earnest this month, with the Fosteriana tulips.

These are to all intents and purposes short, early Darwin types. Fosterianas flower early in the month zestfully coloured in a full range of hues and tones from vivid vermilion (the dreadfully named 'Rockery Beauty') to rich orange ('Orange Emperor') and the almost edible lemon-yellow fading to cream of 'Sweetheart'.

The Early Single tulips are better known for forcing than for growing in the garden, but the tougher varieties are perfectly at home in the open. 'Couleur Cardinal', which is 35cm (14in) tall, is renowned for its vigour and ability to stand up to the weather. It is cardinal red, as you might expect, but deepens to plummy crimson at the bases of the petals. 'Keizerskroon', bicolored in scarlet and yellow, is superb, but needs a bed to itself unless offset by the pure white of 'Diana' or something like 'Apricot Beauty'.

TREES AND SHRUBS

Just occasionally you come across a shrub, or group of shrubs, whose foliage for a short time plays the part of flowers. I do not mean the fickle display of colour that autumn leaves may or may not put on in any particular year, but the reliable show that is an intrinsic part of the development of the leaves of some shrubs.

Pieris are a perfect example. For a period in spring, which varies according to how the season is going, the new leaves on these evergreen shrubs make as dramatic a display of red or pink as any that may be in flower. If they are planted in association with camellias, which is logical, as both genera like the same, leafy, lime-free soils, a richness will be achieved to which camellias on their own could never aspire. Admittedly, the effect may be spoiled by frost, but you take that risk at this time – it is part of gardening.

It is inescapable that those who garden on lime-free soils have by a very long way the best of this month as far as trees and shrubs go. The great spring shrub genera – *Magnolia, Camellia* and *Rhododendron* (which, of course, includes the azaleas that come at the end of the month) – are only available to gardeners on limy soils if they resort to raised beds and containers. Spring for them means concentrating on bulbs, **cherries**, **crab apples**, **berberis**, **daphnes**, **osmanthus** and **viburnums** – all of which will grow on lime-free soil as well. Many are caught out of pocket when they buy the snowy mespilus, **Amelanchier lamarckii.** It is one of the very finest of small trees, bearing its massed white flowers this month, but it must have a lime-free soil.

Japanese cherries (*Prunus* vars), on the other hand, are never entirely happy on moisture-retentive, acid soils. They will grow, flower and attain maturity, but they will also be subject to canker, martyrs to fungus disease, and liable suddenly and dramatically – sometimes when in full flower – to collapse and die. On alkaline, calcareous soils, and especially on chalk, they are much better.

Their peak season is from middle to the end of this month, although some flower earlier and some spill over into next. There are many of them, some of which are too large for the average garden, while a few others are afflictions rather than assets. Among the latter is the egregious 'Kanzan', whose costume is more fitting to a red-light district than to the myriad of suburban streets in which it has been planted at the expense of the unsuspecting public. The great majority, though, offer a feast of delights from which it is not always easy to choose.

Your choices will be between double or single flowers, white or some shade of pink, and rounded or spreading crowns to the trees. Some research will be needed, but here I can only tell you of those that figure highest in my own personal favour. 'Mount Fuji' wins in the double white, spreading class. Its branches are horizontal, eventually bowing towards the ground, and laden with very large, semi-double, pure white blossoms. 'Tai Haku' comes top of the single whites, although it needs a larger than average garden. It is known as the 'Great White Cherry' and has very large, single, white flowers and coppery young foliage. 'Shogetsu', also known as 'Shimidsu Sakura' (Sakura means cherry), is the best spreading tree for small gardens, with a flat crown of branches, all along which hang large, pure white, frilled flowers that open from pink buds. Of the double, pink, 'typical' Japanese Cherries, 'Ichiyo' is almost in a class of its own for delicacy of colouring and general elegance. 'Ama-no-gawa', upright like a little Lombardy poplar and the most widely planted Japanese Cherry of all, has become a cliché and a fairly tiresome one at that.

Camellias are misunderstood beauties, as capable of growing in cold as in mild climates. If you want to see them flower in chilly areas, however, you should choose varieties of *Camellia × williamsii*. In colder climates, such as the north-east of North America, and places with low light levels, such as Scotland, *C. × williamsii* varieties flower freely whereas *C. japonica* varieties tend to fail.

Where the sun is strong camellias should be planted in at least part shade. If you plant any camellia facing the morning sun you will see few flowers, as frosted buds will be killed. Don't plant the bushes where cold winds can reach them, for the simple reason that the plants will die. They are essentially hardy, especially after passing their third year or so, but only in relatively still air.

If your soil is alkaline, you need not exclude all **magnolias**. *Magnolia kobus*, a small tree, will grow on chalk, but rarely flowers until it is between twelve and fifteen years old. Much better are the forms of its hybrid with *M. stellata*, which go under the name *M. × loebneri*. The best known of these is the extremely floriferous 'Leonard Messel', which has flowers like those of *M. stellata*, but lilac-pink. 'Merrill' is becoming more widely known; it is more tree-like and less bushy than 'Leonard Messell', but still small enough as magnolias go. Its flowers, abundantly borne, are pure white. These are two of the best of the smaller magnolias of spring.

MAGNOLIA STELLATA

CAMELLIAS IN THE UNITED KINGDOM
Plant facing south in the north, west in the middle, and north in the south – that is to oversimplify it, but it is not a bad guide.

Camellia × williamsii 'Golden Spangles'

plants
IN
flower

KEY

* = evergreen   spp = species
vars = varieties

NOTES

Arctostaphylos uva-ursi and *Pieris* need lime-free
soil.
Magnolia kobus is good on chalk but does not
flower until 15 years old.

TWICE FLOWERING

The ornamental crab apples are excellent trees for small gardens and give good value, especially if you obtain varieties that flower freely in spring and then bear conspicuous fruits in autumn. *Malus* 'Eleyi' is very popular, with crimson-rose flowers and very fine, deep red fruits. *M.* 'Golden Hornet' has white flowers of good size and its yellow fruits stay on the tree for many weeks.

You can make a crab apple tree 'bloom' twice by growing a clematis into its crown. If you select varieties that do not flower late, you will avoid detracting from the impact of the fruit. Try the crimson 'Mme Edouard André', the light blue 'Perle d'Azur' or the soft pink 'Comtesse de Bouchaud', which flower throughout summer.

Once you realise the benefits of growing clematis into trees you will soon find many other combinations. One of the great advantages is that you can forget about how to prune the clematis – there is no need.

TREES	colour	flower type
Amelanchier lamarckii	White	Racemes along branches
Magnolia kobus	White	Small chalice, scented
liliiflora	Purple outside, cream inside	Slender, erect
liliiflora 'Nigra'	Rich purple	Slender, erect
× *loebneri* 'Merrill'	White	Star shaped, scented
'Leonard Messel'	Lilac pink	Star shaped
× *soulangeana* vars	Various	Large chalice
stellata	White or pink	Star shaped
Malus vars (Ornamental crab apple)	Various	Like apple blossom
Prunus many (Japanese cherries)	Various	
Pyrus salicifolia 'Pendula'	White	Like pear blossom
SHRUBS		
**Arbutus andrachne*	White	Urn shaped
**Arctostaphylos uva-ursi*	White, tinged pink	Urn shaped
**Berberis darwinii*	Orange	Drooping clusters
* × *lologensis*	Orange	Clusters
**Camellia japonica* many vars	Various	Various
* × *williamsii* most vars	Various	Various
Chaenomeles speciosa and C. × *superba* vars	White, pink, red or orange-red	Saucer shaped
Corylopsis pauciflora, C. spicata, C. sinensis (syn. *C. willmottiae*)	Yellow	Hanging clusters
Cytisus praecox 'Warminster'	Rich cream	Massed, pea shaped
*Daphne blagayana	White	Clusters, scented
* × *napolitana*	Rose pink	Clusters, scented
*Erica carnea – later vars	Various	
'Myretoun Ruby'	Ruby red	Bell shaped, racemes
'Vivellii'	Deep carmine, bronze foliage	Bell shaped, long racemes
*Erica × *darleyensis* 'A.T. Johnson'	Magenta	Bell shaped, racemes
Forsythia	Yellow	Star shaped
Kerria japonica	Yellow	Single and double forms
**Mahonia aquifolium*	Yellow	Terminal clusters
*Osmanthus × *burkwoodii*	White	Small
* *delavayi*	White	Small

	colour	flower type
Pieris – many vars	White	Urn shaped
Rhododendron – many spp and vars	Various	
Ribes (Flowering currant)	Pink	Hanging clusters
***Skimmia japonica* 'Foremannii'**	White	Small, scented
Viburnum × burkwoodii vars	White	Large, clusters, scented
carlesii	White or pink	Large clusters, scented

PERENNIALS

	colour	height
Bergenia	White, red or pink	30–40cm (12–16in)
***Caltha palustris* 'Plena'** (Double marsh mallow)	Yellow	30cm (12in)
***Doronicum* 'Miss Mason'**	Yellow	45cm (18in)
Epimedium perralderianum	Bronze yellow	25cm (10in)
Euphorbia polychroma	Sulphur yellow	45cm (18in)
Helleborus foetidus	Citron, maroon edge	45cm (18in)
orientalis	Various from white to purple	40cm (16in)
Lamium maculatum vars	White spikes	15cm (6in)
Omphalodes cappadocica	Blue	15cm (6in)
Peltiphyllum peltatum	Pink, before large leaves	1m (40in)
***Primula* 'Wanda'**	Wine purple	10cm (4in)
Saxifraga umbrosa	Pink	15cm (6in)

BULBS

Anemone nemorosa	White	10cm (4in)
Corydalis solida	Purple-pink	15cm (6in)
Tulips – ***fosteriana*** and ***greigii*** types	Various	Various
Erythroniums	Yellow, white or lilac	12–30cm (5–12in)
Fritillaria meleagris	Various	22cm (9in)
Daffodils and **narcissi** many	Yellows, white	Various
Muscari spp	Blue or white	12–30cm (5–12in)

ROCK GARDEN BULBS

Narcissus 'Hawera'	Lemon-yellow	15cm (6in)
'Lintie'	Yellow, orange-cupped	15cm (6in)
'Pipit'	Light lemon and white	25cm (10in)

SCENTS OF SPRING

The scented shrubs of spring are more noticeable than the ones that came into flower during the winter months, but only because you are there to catch their perfumes instead of inside by the fire. Nevertheless, they are among the most deliciously fragrant of all and are not to be missed.

When planting, remember that this is a showery month and put the shrubs where you can enjoy them fully. It is most frustrating to catch a waft of perfume and not be able to get nearer because of not wanting to tread on sodden ground. If you do not already grow *Osmanthus* × *burkwoodii*, *O. delavayi*, *Viburnum* × *burkwoodii* or one of the varieties of *V. carlesii* such as 'Aurora', make a note now to do so – and to find just the right position.

A CARPET OF BULBS

One of the most effective ways of growing spring bulbs is round the bases of trees. Close to the trunks, the roots are deep and are acting as anchors rather than actively feeding. You can quite safely plant bulbs in the pockets of soil between the main roots, and it is perfectly in order to add organic matter to the soil to give the bulbs a good start. All spring bulbs, including erythroniums – the gorgeous trout lilies and avalanche lilies from America and the dog's tooth violet from Europe – can be grown in this way.

If you have trees as lawn specimens and keep a circle of clean soil round the base of each one, make use of the space by planting it with bulbs such as *Fritillaria meleagris*, the snakes head fritillary. It grows to about 20cm (8in) and bears nodding flowers like cloche hats. They always have a reticulate pattern of veining, and are prettily and modestly coloured in shades of purple-red, purple-pink and white.

ROCK GARDEN

Adonis vernalis
Alyssum saxatile 'Compactum'
Aubrieta
Haberlea
Primula auricula vars
Primula marginata vars
Pulsatilla vulgaris
Ramonda myconii

M A Y

Whan that the month of May
Is comen, and that I here the foules singe,
And that the floures ginnen for to springe,
Farwel my book and my devocioun!

CHAUCER

This is the month of freshness and perfection. Everything in the garden looks forward fearlessly to the future and there is none of the hedging of horticultural bets that goes on later, when the rush to discard flowers and concentrate on setting seed sets in. Flowers have a boisterous glow and only the insensitive fail to detect the burgeoning celebration of the return of warm weather.

Early in the month, however, it is still possible to find that a sharp reminder of winter has browned a magnolia or reduced rhododendron flowerheads to a pulpy mass. On the whole, though, this is the time when you can relax and think about planting out tender subjects that you could not risk before.

Now is the height of the shrub season. It is all too easy to fall for the beauty of the late spring garden, to the extent that you fill it with the bounty of spring and leave no room for the other seasons, but restraint must prevail. The nature of your garden will to some extent make your choice for you. If you garden on a soil with lime in it, the world of rhododendrons, deciduous azaleas and their allies is closed to you, but for an occasional favourite in a tub. Never mind, you only have to visit some of the largest gardens to see how drab in later months an over-emphasis on one group can be, and the richness of the late spring allows you full rein without them.

This is the gardening month. Enthusiasm swings to great heights, but we must beware of summer ennui. Month by month our gardens flower; let us enjoy the late spring festival, but let us also remember that it is but one twelfth of the year. There is much more to come.

tasks

FOR THE

month
1

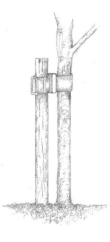

CHECKLIST

- ☐ Watch out for late frosts
- ☐ Harden off all plants raised under glass before planting them out
- ☐ Plant out early chrysanthemums towards the end of the month
- ☐ Prune camellias if necessary
- ☐ Check all tree ties
- ☐ Check rhododendrons for signs of disease
- ☐ Look out for the first signs of greenfly on roses and start regular spraying. Remove any suckers
- ☐ Keep a strict eye out for slugs, especially around developing hostas and delphiniums
- ☐ Plant magnolias and water-lilies

MAINTENANCE

LATE FROSTS

Although this is indeed the time for beginning to put out tender plants, hanging baskets and so on, it pays never to be too complacent – frosts can strike surprisingly late. On the other hand, gardeners cannot afford to be too pessimistic, either, otherwise they would find themselves never getting anything done. Keep a sharp eye on the weather forecasts – tune in to the forecasts for farmers – and have contingency plans ready (a clear space in the shed for baskets, for example.

WARNING

■ *A damaging frost can set you back an entire year, destroying 'geraniums' (pelargoniums), fuchsias and the half-hardy annuals you have gone to the trouble of raising* ■

CAMELLIAS

If you are growing camellias in containers – tubs, barrels and so on – as you may well be if your garden soil is limy, survey them for top-heaviness and for odd branches that grow out of balance. In the open ground the plant would set itself to rights over the next couple of years, but container growing demands more immediate discipline. If you cut back now, while new growth is still active, some restoration of balance will take place. Leave it much longer and extension growth will stop (this happens usually towards the middle of next month).

TREE TIES

Try to find time this month to check all your tree ties. The wilder winds of the year should be over, and this is the period when you should remove ties from trees and taller shrubs that have become firmly anchored. Those that need to remain

for a further year should be examined and tightened if they have worn loose, or loosened if they have become too tight because of the growth in diameter of the stems.

It is not only false economy but folly to attempt to economise on tree ties by using string, nylon stockings, strips of rubber inner tube, or any of the gimcrack efforts seen in the gardens of otherwise intelligent people. Nylon string cuts into the stems as they expand, creating a groove which is such a source of weakness that it is an absolute certainty that the stem will eventually snap. Stockings or panty-hose do exactly the same, and have the added disadvantage of combining untidiness with a distinct air of the ridiculous. Gadgets made with rubber strips merely give with the motion of the tree stems and cause abrasions.

It is hard to understand how gardeners can invest ten per cent of the average weekly industrial wage on a tree and then abjure the few pennies it costs to ensure its proper development.

RHODODENDRON DISEASES

Rhododendrons of several kinds, but most particularly the Cinnabarina subsection of the genus, which includes the 'Lady Roseberry' and 'Lady Chamberlain' groups, must be regarded as vulnerable to rhododendron powdery mildew. Bi-weekly spraying with a systemic fungicide, starting in early spring and continuing until late autumn, should prevent its appearance. Branches showing the symptoms should be removed and burnt. If this disease is left unchecked, the entire shrub becomes leafless and dies.

It is not a good idea to exclude any particular group of rhododendrons from your garden. As time goes by it will be found that a large number of species and hybrids will become infected. As the disease spreads to encompass hitherto unaffected areas of the country, preventive treatment will increasingly become the rule, rather than the exception.

Rhododendron bud blast is another disease that is gradually widening its geographical range. This manifests itself in blackening of the flowerbuds, which then grow what appear to be black whiskers and are in fact the fruiting bodies of the infecting fungus. You can pick off all such buds early in the year, taking care to touch none that are free of the disease, and burn them. My experience is that you will be putting off the inevitable and it is probably better to dig up affected plants and consign them to the bonfire, as one or two blackened buds, missed in the picking off, can infect several more bushes through their windborne spores. It is not easy, however, to bring yourself to destroy a mature shrub with just a few infected buds.

● ROSES

Examine all your roses, especially those that have been planted for about three years, for suckers.
Left alone they will take over and destroy the rose. The purpose of doing this job now is to remove the suckers while they are still young, tender and manageable; leave them until later and they will have become tough, rendering the roses liable to damage when you attack the suckers.

PLANTING

● MAGNOLIAS

This is an excellent month in which to plant magnolias. They have tender, fleshy roots that are easily damaged, and if this happens in autumn or earlier in the spring they do not regenerate and the plant is liable to start on a slow decline. Far too many gardeners find themselves bewildered by the 'going backwards' exhibited by their magnolias and think they cannot grow them, whereas it is merely a matter of understanding their needs.

Cultivate an area 1m (1yd) square to a depth of one spit (spade's depth) and a half.

■ Dig it over thoroughly and incorporate generous quantities of moss peat as a conditioner. Magnolias love soft but firm going in their early years and can penetrate heavier soils only when they are older.

■ Use one of the short-stake methods of support (see page 151). It will allow the magnolia to be held firmly against rocking but will not involve disturbance of the root ball.

● WATER-LILIES

This is also the best month for planting water-lilies.

Your supplier will give you advice about which sorts of lily pots or crates to use (they depend on the variety of water-lily), about compost, and concerning the proper depth for each plant, but the most important point is that they must not be planted to their full depth straight away.

Water-lily leaf stalks grow to the precise depth of the water they are in, but can only do so relatively slowly. Put the new plants in too deeply and the leaves will die. The way to overcome this is to put the pot fairly near to the edge of the pond and over a period of several days gradually move it further into deep water. Alternatively, you can set the pot on stones or bricks and remove one at a time until the plant is at its optimum depth.

PLANTING MAGNOLIAS

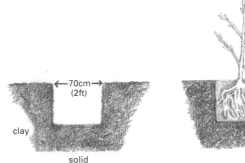

←70cm→ (2ft)

clay

solid

WRONG

RIGHT

plants
OF THE
month
1

AZALEA
Deciduous Azaleas

These are quite different from the Japanese azaleas. They are much taller and lose their leaves in winter, almost always with a dazzling display of autumn foliage colour. Their branch structure is more open and their flowers are a good deal larger, typically open-trumpet shaped, and their colour range is wider and more flamboyant, including brilliant orange and many shades of yellow. Some varieties, however, are more restrained.

type	Deciduous shrubs
flowers	A wide range of colours
foliage	Leaves 10–12cm (4–5in) long, not broad. Light green
height	1.5m (5ft) after 10 years
spread	1m (3ft) after 10 years
hardiness	Hardy
position	Full sun or part shade
soil	Lime-free, peaty or leafy, moisture-retentive soil
pruning	None
propagation	By cuttings. Heat and artificial light are essential; not a subject for home gardeners to try

PRIMULA
Primula 'Guinevere'

A primula with a character all of its own. It is also known as *P.* 'Garryarde Guinevere' and was one of a series of 'Garryarde' hybrids, of which it is now virtually the sole survivor. It is easily grown and increases well. Its great virtues are the freedom with which it produces its flowers, their unique shade of soft, carmine pink, and the beautiful bronze foliage – as desirable a ground-cover feature as one could wish.

type	Herbaceous perennial
flowers	Almost stemless, carmine-pink with yellow 'eye'
foliage	Rugose (wrinkled), varied shades of deep green-bronze
height	10cm (4in)
spread	To 30cm (1ft)
hardiness	Hardy
planting	Avoid planting primulas in summer – otherwise any time in suitable weather
position	Part shade
soil	Any good garden soil. Soils over chalk should not be too shallow
propagation	By division after flowering. Plant the larger divisions immediately and pot up the small ones to grow on in a frame
alternatives	There are many primulas, but none like 'Guinevere'

VIBURNUM
Viburnum plicatum 'Mariesii'

The 'wedding cake' virburnum is aptly nicknamed. The horizontal branches, wreathed in heads of flowers all along their length, have a tiered effect that is unmistakable. It is an easy plant to grow but has an air of quality that suggests an aristocratic ancestry. Its attractiveness is by no means confined to flowering time.

type	Deciduous shrub
flowers	White, in heads somewhat similar to those of a 'lacecap' hydrangea
fruits	Black, not often borne
foliage	Softly green, pleated (hence *plicatum*). Quite good autumn colour in some years
height	2m (7ft) after 10 years
spread	2m (7ft) after 10 years
hardiness	Hardy
position	Part shade
soil	Any good garden soil

DECIDUOUS AZALEA SEEDLING

PRIMULA 'GUINEVERE'

pruning	None
propagation	Semi-ripe cuttings taken in summer require heat at 21°C (70°F). Hardwood cuttings taken in late autumn may be rooted in a garden frame
alternatives	*V.p.* 'Lanarth' is stronger growing. 'Pink Beauty' has flowers that become blushed with pink as they age. 'Rowallane' bears its fruits freely

CLEMATIS
Clematis 'Nelly Moser'

'Nelly Moser' has become the classic clematis, but it is only one of many that have a first flush of flowers in late spring to early summer, followed by another in late summer to early autumn. It is not realised often enough that 'Nelly Moser' fades badly in sun and is the ideal clematis for growing on a shady wall.

type	Deciduous climber, requiring support
flowers	Large, lilac-pink with carmine-pink bar: two flushes each year
foliage	Mid-green
height	2.5m (9ft)

spread	Varies with training
hardiness	Hardy
position	Full or part shade – out of strong sun
soil	Any good garden soil. Make a 30cm (1ft) cube planting hole and fill the bottom with well-rotted manure and the rest with rich, friable soil
pruning	This variety has its first flush of flowers on wood made the previous year and should therefore not be pruned heavily in spring. After flowering, cut back the old flowering wood, taking care not to damage the wood that will flower the next year
propagation	By internodal cuttings in summer. Difficult
alternatives	Several. Choice becomes a matter of colour as between varieties enjoying similar conditions
special comment	Great care should be taken not to allow the stems of clematis to buckle, particularly during planting and pruning. Buckling causes damage that allows the ingress of the clematis wilt fungus

M A Y

57

tasks
FOR THE
month
2

Even though the rock garden may be at its best for flowering, it may well be approaching its peak as a source of softwood cuttings

PROPAGATION

SOFTWOOD CUTTINGS OF ALPINES

A very large number of alpine plants can be propagated from cuttings of soft wood at this time of year. Whereas the majority of garden shrubs are best increased by semi-ripe cuttings from mid- to late summer, this is the preferred method for alpines.

The cuttings are taken when they are just large enough to handle. They may be anything from 2.5cm (1in) long or more in shrubby penstemons and many dianthus, to as little as 1.5mm ($\frac{1}{16}$in) in cushion plants such as dionysias.

Softwood cuttings do not require artificial heat. They root extremely rapidly if you take them just at the right stage and give them the right conditions. The idea is to allow them sufficient natural heat, while at the same time shading them from sun scorch.

Taking softwood cuttings

Phlox douglasii 'Boothman's Variety' is a good example of a typical subject. You should look for cuttings material not just immediately flowering is over, but while the last few flowers are still out. The plant makes a neat, slightly domed mat of mid-green foliage with a greyish tint. Peeping between the stems you will see fresh, bright green ones, and if you part the plant you will find that they are about 1.8cm ($\frac{3}{4}$in) long.

Take an extremely sharp knife or razor blade – I use a surgical scalpel – and make a neat horizontal cut to remove the cutting just below its lowest leaf joint. Put the cutting into a plastic bag and close the neck. I usually put the neck of the bag under my foot. Then move on across the plant, until you have all the cuttings you want.

Preparing the cuttings

Take your blade and, cutting down onto a block of wood, cut away the lowest pair of leaves flush with, but not so as to damage, the stem. Longer cuttings may need to have the next pair up removed as well. Preparing soft cuttings by pulling off the leaves tears the tender bark of the stems; cutting with a razor-sharp blade while the cutting is held in the hand is just plain stupid.

Inserting cuttings in the rooting medium

Use clay pots. Plastic ones distort when lifted and can disturb the fine, new roots. Place an inverted crock over

the drainage hole. This is to prevent the compost running out and, as you are going to use pure sand, it is most important.

Fill the pot with silver sand or any other sharp sand, but not fine builder's sand. Immerse the lower part of the pot in water and wait until the surface of the pot darkens.

Now, using a dibber the size of a matchstick, insert the cuttings in the sand so that no two touch one another and no single cutting fails to have its base in contact with the sand. Place the pot in a frame.

Frames for softwood cuttings

An ordinary garden frame, facing the sun but shaded with netting to about 50 per cent, will provide heat and enough light to root the cuttings quickly. They will need to be lightly and carefully watered with a fine rose at least twice a day. If you are away from home all day, place the frame in a less sunny position.

Potting up the cuttings

Test the cuttings by tugging very gently indeed. When most appear to have rooted, lift them out with care, one at a time, and plant them in 8cm (3¼in) pots in a soil-based potting compost. Sand has no food value, so pot up the cuttings as soon after rooting as possible.

Difficult cuttings

Alpine gardeners who want to try their hand at difficult subjects like dionysias should take the new rosettes as they emerge from between the leaves of the old ones and remove them with a keen blade. Handling must be so gentle as to cause no bruising. Place the cuttings, which may be extremely tiny, in sand which has previously been watered and is in a propagating tray. The

lid of the tray should have ventilators in it. Replace the lid with the ventilators open and put the whole propagator at the foot of a shady wall. Cover the ventilators with small, flat stones or pieces of slate so that air can get in but not rain. The sand must never be watered again and should stay damp for six weeks or more, by which time the cuttings will have rooted or rotted. Potting on is tricky and you can expect 50 per cent losses.

Rooting times

Such a long rooting time is exceptional. Most softwood alpine cuttings will root within two weeks or a little longer. I have on occasion rooted alpine phloxes in as little as four days, but that is also exceptional.

PLANNING

PLANNING BORDERS

Many gardeners make the mistake of neglecting to plan ahead at this time of year. There is so much to do, so many good things to enjoy, and it does not feel like a planning time at all.

Nevertheless, you should not take your eye off the ball. No sooner has this period passed than you will find yourself embroiled in school or family holidays or both, followed by the scramble to recover from them, and suddenly autumn is upon you.

This is why you see so many badly planned herbaceous borders. Start thinking about a new one (or even refurbishing the existing one) now, and you will have the whole summer to go round looking at other people's borders and appropriating the best ideas for plants and colour associations.

CUTTING FROM ALPINES

With most of the alpines that can be propagated from cuttings, the cuttings are best taken at the softwood stage. Some, however, should be taken later, when they are half ripe (see p90); among these are aubrieta, most dwarf shrubs and dwarf conifers

CLEAN CONTAINERS

No matter what technique you are using or what the pots or trays are made of, always take time to wash containers for cuttings or seed in advance. A dilute solution of a mild antiseptic will help to promote hygiene. Make sure the pots are dry before you fill them with compost, otherwise you will find the job becomes messy.

GAPS IN THE BORDER

If gaps appear where herbaceous plants have failed to come up after their winter rest, mark the centre of the space with a slender cane to which you have attached a label. Then plant the space with annuals. Nicotiana 'Lime Green' is a good one of which to have a stock, as its colour goes with everything and it is tall and robust enough to compete with the perennials.

M A Y

plants
OF THE
month
2

▼ RHODODENDRON
Rhododendron 'Lady Rosebery'

This is in fact a group of rhododendrons, all of which have similarly shaped flowers in rich shades of pink. The 'Lady Chamberlain' group have the same type of flowers but with more or less orange in their red. The many-flowered clusters are unmistakable because of the long, narrowly bell-shaped blooms and their waxy texture.

type	Evergreen shrub
flowers	Clusters of six or more, pink to carmine, waxy
foliage	Distinctive: long-oval, sea-green
height	2m (7ft) after 10 years
spread	1.25m (4ft) after 10 years
hardiness	Hardy
position	Part shade
soil	Must be lime free, leafy or peaty, and moisture retentive
pruning	None
propagation	Semi-ripe summer cuttings will root in a mist unit
alternatives	The 'Lady Chamberlain' group
special comment	These groups of rhododendrons are susceptible to rhododendron powdery mildew. This disease has only occurred in recent years, but is spreading and potentially lethal. The symptoms are irregular, greyish-purple patches, not to be confused with frost damage. Spraying with a systemic fungicide as a preventive is the best course of action

LILAC
Syringa × josiflexa 'Bellicent'

Syringa is the lilac genus. The well-known, large-clustered varieties can be seen perhaps too much during late spring and lose something of the grace of the species. 'Bellicent' is sufficiently close to nature to show the daintiness and charm of species lilacs while putting on a sumptuous show

type	Deciduous large shrub or small tree
flowers	Large panicles of rose-pink; fragrant
foliage	Fine, deep green leaves
height	2.5m (9ft) after 10 years
spread	1.5–2m (5–7ft) after 10 years
hardiness	Hardy (raised in Ottawa)
position	Sun or part shade
soil	All good, well-drained soils, especially happy on chalk
pruning	Remove the old flowering wood after flowering. This, however, is not as essential as it is with the usual garden hybrids, and suckering is not a problem
propagation	Best by semi-ripe cuttings taken in summer with a heel of old wood and rooted in a heated propagator 18°C (65°F)
alternatives	*Syringa x persica* (Persian lilac); similar, but with smaller panicles
special comment	*Syringa* is the correct generic name for lilacs. Philadelphus, though often called 'syringas', are entirely different (see p.81)

WEIGELA
Weigela Hybrids

The most rewarding weigelas (pronounced wi'jeel'ias) are the selected hybrids, of which there are about thirty. They vary in flower colour but are reliable, free-flowering shrubs for late spring and early summer. They are of easy culture, although attention should be paid to pruning if flowering is to remain free and the shrubs are not to grow too large.

RHODODENDRON 'LADY ROSEBERY'

type	Deciduous shrub
flowers	Red, white, or shades of pink
foliage	Ovate-oblong, smallish leaves with tapered points
height	1.5m (5ft) after 10 years
spread	1.3m (4½ft) after 10 years
hardiness	Hardy
position	Full sun or a little shade
soil	Any good garden soil
pruning	Immediately flowering is over, shorten or remove the old flowering shoots and shorten any over-long branches that may unbalance the shrub
propagation	Semi-ripe cuttings taken in late summer will root in heat at 21°C (70°F), or softwood cuttings taken in early summer will root in a garden frame
varieties	'Abel Carrière' – carmine, 'Eva Rathke' – crimson, 'Looymansii Aurea' – pink, gold foliage, *W. florida* 'Variegata' – pink with cream-edged foliage

CEANOTHUS
Ceanothus × veitchianus

Ceanothus are known as Californian Lilacs. That they come from California may alert those of us in colder climates to a suspicion of tenderness, but the 'lilac' sobriquet is misleading; ceanothus and lilacs are not related. They can be evergreen or deciduous, there is a small-leaved group and one with considerably larger leaves, the flowers can be blue, pink or white, although the majority are in shades of blue. This hybrid is the hardiest, and the most prolific with its flowers.

type	Evergreen shrub
flowers	Clusters of rich blue
foliage	Small, slightly wrinkled, wedge-shaped leaves
height	1.25m (4ft) after 10 years
spread	1.5m (5ft) after 10 years
hardiness	Hardy in all but the coldest places
position	Full sun or a little shade
soil	Ceanothus are lime-tolerant but do not do well on shallow, chalky soils. Good drainage is essential
pruning	None
propagation	Semi-ripe cuttings taken in summer require heat at 21°C (70°F) or a mist unit
alternatives	'Blue Mound' (deciduous, light blue); 'Cascade' (evergreen, bright blue); *impressus* (evergreen, dense habit, dark blue, hardy in

CEANOTHUS × VEITCHIANUS

shelter); 'Puget Blue' (evergreen, very long-flowering, deep blue). All flower late spring to early summer

practical project

CREATING A GARDEN POND

DON'T RUSH
A garden pond should be regarded as a living, balanced, co-operating entity. Do not be in too much of a rush to see it achieve stability.

FINDING THE LEVEL
Water finds its own level. If you do not get the rim of the pond perfectly level, the liner will be exposed in the shallow areas and will eventually split through the action of ultra-violet light. Knock in pegs round the pond's edge and use a spirit level to make sure all is well. If it is not, build up the low places and lower the high ones.

Water-lilies are among the most spectacular flowers we can grow in temperate climates, and they are among the glories of the summer garden. You must have water for them to grow in and, unless you are going to restrict yourself to the very small ones, you will have to consider making a pond for them and some other water and marginal plants – including oxygenating plants, which are essential.

There are several ways in which you can make a pond, but let us assume you would like it to look as natural as possible and have decided to excavate it, rather than build it up from ground level. As the great majority of garden ponds are made with liners these days, especially now that butyl materials have become so tough and reliable, there is little point in going to the trouble, expense and back-breaking labour of attempting to line your pond with concrete.

This is the perfect month for the job, as it is the ideal time for planting water plants and the soil will be much drier and lighter than it was earlier. Furthermore, it should not yet be too hot for a good bout of manual labour.

DESIGNING THE POND

Make sure that the site you have chosen is the right one, and then look again to make sure – it is rather late to change your mind after you have moved several cubic metres of earth. The pond should not be on any sort of rise in the ground, otherwise it will look silly – ponds rarely occur on humps, and most usually in hollows. If you are going to rob the lawn to make the pond, ensure that the area of water will be in proportion, and try if you can to relate it to other features such as a rock garden or even a curve in the lawn's boundary.

When designing your pond, do not forget that you cannot step into it without damaging the liner. Make sure, therefore, that you make it of a size and shape that will allow you access to its entire surface.

■ Take a length of hose, a rope, or a few dozen small plastic pots and mark out the shape of the pond on the soil or grass. If you use this method you can adjust the shape until you have got it just right. Take a look from an upstairs window; it is surprising how much better you can judge proportion from above.

■ Decide, too, at this early stage how you want the surrounds of the pond to look. Do you want a rock garden to come right down to the water's edge? Perhaps you would like an informally paved path right round.

POND SIZE

Try to make the largest pond you can, and make sure it is deep enough. Small, shallow ponds are almost useless, as they can freeze to the bottom, killing fish, they are likely to become soupy with algae, and the range of plants you can grow is very limited.

CALCULATING LINER SIZE

A pond up to 2.75sq m (3½sq yd) in area should be no less than 38cm (15in) deep. From 2.75 to 11sq m (3½ to 14sq yd) it should be 45cm (18in) deep, between 11 and 22sq m (14 and 28sq yd) the depth should be 60cm (2ft), and anything over that size should have 75cm (2½ft) depth of water – the maximum that is necessary, even for a small lake.

To work out what size of liner you need, measure the length and width of the pond at their widest points. For a circle, measure the diameter. Add twice the maximum depth of the pond to each measurement. Then: Area of liner = (maximum length + twice maximum depth) × (maximum width + twice maximum depth). For a circular pond, the area is (diameter + twice the maximum depth)².

Do not dig straight down at the sides, but make them sloping, with a shelf 22cm (9in) deep and 30cm (1ft) wide round the rim of the pond. On this you will be able to stand pots of marginal plants so that their root balls are just covered with water. The shelf makes no difference to the area of liner required.

LINING AND FILLING THE POND

When excavation is complete, make sure no sharp objects such as stones or roots are liable to abrade the liner, and make doubly certain by first lining the hole with a layer of sand about 2.5cm (1in) deep.

Now lay in the liner so that it is evenly spread, and weigh it down with bricks or stones placed outside the rim of the excavation. Let water in gently, moving the stones to allow the liner to settle, and gently but firmly pulling out most of the creases that form. A few creases are inevitable.

When the pond is full, let it settle for a day or so and then trim off the surplus lining, leaving a flap about 15cm (6in) wide. This can be anchored and disguised using rocks, paving stones, or whatever you decided earlier.

It is essential to let the pond stand empty for a few days to allow the water to detoxify. Most water supplies deliver unwanted chemicals – chlorine and so on – and you should give them a chance to clear.

PLANTING THE POND

Your very first planting job will be to introduce oxygenating plants. Make sure there are plenty, and allow them ten days or so to begin to do their work. If you plant too few you will find you are battling against algae, including the dreaded blanket weed.

Next, plant your water-lilies and other aquatics, and then, as the very last thing, introduce any fish you have decided to keep, but at far less than the stocking rate you might have thought appropriate. Introduce too many fish too soon and the ecological balance of your pond will be spoilt. Fish produce droppings, which are acted upon by bacteria to produce nitrates. These nitrates are then used by the plants in the pond as food, which prevents them from building up to poisonous levels. If the bacteria have not had time to build up to an effective population they will not be able to break down the droppings quickly enough and your pond will not be healthy.

OXYGENATING PLANTS

A selection for your pond:

Callitriche autumnalis

Callitriche verna (starwort)

Ceratophyllum demersum

Eleocharis acicularis (hairgrass)

Elodea canadensis (Canadian pond weed)

Hottonia palustris (water violet)

Myriophyllum verticillatum

Myriophyllum spicatum

Ranunculus aquatilis (water buttercup)

plant
selections

Euphorbia griffithii
'Fireglow'

BULBS

There are all sorts of fancy **tulips** that can tempt you from the pages of bulb catalogues: Viridifloras with green bands central to the petals; Parrot tulips like twisted blobs of oil paint, and Frilled tulips – really Parrot types with fringes – confections that would put Ascot hats to shame. There can be little forgiveness for some of the names, too. 'Gay Presto' indeed!

But the Darwin tulips – those of the elegant, uncomplicated, square-based goblet shape – and their oval cousins, the Cottage tulips, are aristocrats among the flowers of late spring. You can grow them in substantial clumps, in formal arrangements, or even in closely packed drifts at the side of the lawn – where you should arrange for sweetly curved outlines and never a sharp corner.

ALPINES

The rock garden now takes on a stronger palette entirely appropriate to the greater intensity of light. At one month from the summer solstice the light is almost at its brightest, and we tend to forget this and try to perpetuate the soft colours of spring.

Mat-forming hybrids of **Phlox subulata** in anything from softest pink to the most flaring magenta take over from the aubrietas, and **helianthemums**, whose Mediterranean appearance is the real thing, introduce heady orange and the flame tones of red, as well as a leavening of cream and soft yellow.

Helianthemums are not plants to be planted and then ignored. When their flowering finishes next month, do not let them relax, but cut them hard back. They will put on bushy new growth and flower again on the new wood late in the summer. This treatment will also keep them green and compact instead of allowing them to become a sprawl of woody stems just waiting to entangle the heels of potentially litigious visitors.

HERBACEOUS PERENNIALS

In the more 'woodsy' parts of the garden, one of the true blues among ground-hugging plants keeps modestly low but impresses by the freedom with which it bears its round, light royal-blue flowers. **Omphalodes cappadocica** is one of the minor glories of later spring which, if not included among the more obvious stars, renders their performance less rich. Lighter blue and almost as self-effacing, are the spring **veronicas** – *V. teucrium* 'Royal Blue' and *V. gentianoides* – perfect in front of the soft pink, 60cm (2ft) *Pyrethrum* 'Eileen May Robinson'.

Euphorbias dance to a different drum. Their odd flowers mass together to create effects that are simultaneously warm and cool. Nothing else does this in quite the same way. *Euphorbia griffithii* 'Fireglow' has cool green foliage and heads of bracts in a muted, warmish orange-red that is nevertheless conspicuous. *E. myrsinites* is of a greenish, staring yellow that should be offensive but is anything but. There is somehow a softness that saves it from vulgarity.

TREES AND SHRUBS

In colder areas, **rhododendron** time arrives, having been delayed until the later frosts are no longer a danger. The Hardy Hybrids – red 'Doncaster', 'Cynthia' and 'Lord Roberts'; purple-blue 'Blue Peter' and many others – should be chosen with infinite care, as they become large and have little to recommend them for the rest of the year, but among rhododendrons that flower now there are so many species and varieties that there are some for everyone.

Late spring is **hawthorn** time – so much so that in old England it was called 'May' and you were supposed never to 'cast a clout' (discard winter clothing) until 'May be out' (hawthorn in blossom). Hawthorns and other thorns are excellent value for smaller gardens, especially those with pink or red flowers, and have, of course, their fruits with which to decorate themselves later in the year.

The **beauty bush**, *Kolkwitzia amabilis*, covers itself in lipped, pink flowers in late spring and early summer. There is a selected form called 'Pink Cloud' that is worth seeking out, but beware: unscrupulous hands may attach such a label to ordinary forms and charge you more. Not that the 'ordinary' versions of this lovely plant are to be despised, but a deal is a deal. You can grow smaller clematis into this shrub; try the tulip-shaped flowers of the Texensis group of clematis. My favourite is 'Gravetye Beauty', a sensation in ruby red that will dress the beauty bush in rich finery in late summer and early autumn. This is no mean device for enlivening shrubs with but one season of flower and not much to offer in the foliage line.

The utterly delicious **Mexican orange blossom**, *Choisya ternata*, is increasingly becoming known for its hardiness. Its glossy, dainty foliage is attractive all year round and because it is evergreen it must be out of cold winds, but for a plant whose home is south of the Tropic of Cancer, it is truly remarkable. It will produce its main crop of sweetly scented, white flowers now, but there will hardly be a month in which it does not carry a few blooms.

petunias and their ilk can play their part in integrating house and garden and in making you feel that you are really justified in putting away your woollens.

To do justice to the magical time that bridges spring and summer is impossible within the confines of this space. Perhaps, appetite whetted, you will go and see for yourself what riches there are. Do not, however, fill your garden with this month's delights. Be selective, choose the best for your tastes and gardening conditions, and difficult though it may be, remember that there are eleven other months.

(left) The 'English' bluebell is native to much of Europe

(below) As the danger of frost passes, hanging baskets may be put out with impunity

WILD FLOWERS

Not everything in the garden needs to be exotic. While few of the wild flowers native to the country in which one gardens tend to be good garden plants, some do, and in Britain the native bluebell – *Hyacinthoides non-scripta* – is reliable, safe, and one of the most romantic flowers of all. It is by nature a plant of the woodland floor, and such positions suit it well, but it will grow perfectly happily in a considerable amount of sun. However, the best way of all to enjoy it is to see it assert itself among the freshly unfurled leaves of hostas. Its own foliage lies almost flat, but in borrowing that of other, well-chosen subjects, it becomes a plant of many guises.

TENDER PLANTS

Towards the end of the month you can begin to indulge your passion for tender plants. Hanging baskets of lobelias, 'geraniums',

J U N E

What is so rare as a day in June?
Then, if ever, come perfect days.
JAMES RUSSELL LOWELL

*Early summer days can be truly perfect, with skies of a powder
blue as yet unsullied by dust or wearied by having to get up early
every morning. The longest day of the year comes this month, and
after a short pause the nights begin to 'draw in'. And yet this is not
high summer, but only its beginning. The season has not yet
learned its craft and is all too wont to lose concentration and
relapse into greyness and torrential rain.*

*This is no bad thing for the gardener who, knowing that dry times
are to come, welcomes the freshening downpours that keep the
colours of the earlier perennials clean and bright. Delphiniums
and oriental poppies have a jewel-like quality in their best blues
and sweetest pinks, and lupins make the best of their summer
dresses before the senior matrons of the border take precedence.
On the whole it is not a colourful time for shrubs. There is an
early summer 'gap', during which the grand array of spring-
flowering shrubs are concentrating on making and ripening new
growth and those that have yet to flower wait, for the most part,
until pollinating insects have done with the herbaceous flowers.
Flowers, we may think, were created for our pleasure, but it is not
so. They exist solely and single-mindedly to induce pollination, so
that seed may be set and the species preserved.*

*It is hard, though, to think of such things during a balmy early
summer evening, when scents are borne on the lightest airs, bees
hum their soporific drone, and birds play a little music before
bedtime. This is a good month during which to recall that the best
garden tool is a deck chair, and that time taken to savour the
early summer garden can never be wasted. Is that not after all
what you made the garden for?*

tasks

FOR THE

month

1

CHECKLIST

- Start watering during dry spells, but check the local by-laws and any general restrictions
- Keep pests and diseases under control
- Plant out hardy fuchsias and well-hardened half-hardy annuals
- Deadhead spring-flowering bulbs
- Cut back oriental poppies
- Prune evergreen hedges, broom and *Clematis montana*
- Feed tulips and hyacinths
- Maintain the spraying programme for roses and, later in the month, start deadheading
- If you have used polyanthus for spring bedding, lift them and replant in a cool, moist spot for the summer
- Tie in climbers and wall shrubs

MAINTENANCE

WATERING

It is worth remembering that something like 50 per cent of the water lost by the top 22cm (9in) of soil during a prolonged drought has actually been lost during the first five days. Do not leave watering until plants start to show distress. If you do so, you will be setting them

WARNING

- *Despite the need of your plants for water, if hosepipe and other watering bans or regulations are in force, observe them scrupulously. You may notice others in the neighbourhood who are not doing so, but they are likely to be the poorer for it in the long run* ■

back more severely than you might think and will cause them to suffer from retarded growth and reduced crops of flowers. As you are gardening for flowers, it is important not to let this happen.

PESTS

Early summer is the time when vigilance and self-discipline pay off in the war against pests. It is young plants and the young wood of older ones that are especially vulnerable. Later on, tissues toughen up and become unpalatable to many insects as they become progressively loaded with bitter tannins. If you regard this as the anti-pest month you will find it pays off when you do not have to take remedial action later.

CUTTING BACK

Oriental poppies should be cut down as soon as they

finish flowering. There is no point in letting them set seed. Take sharp shears and cut back the leaves by one half. This makes for neatness and also encourages the formation of new shoots from the base. Untidy poppies spoil the effect of the plants behind that are to follow.

LILY DISEASES

Lilies often suffer from virus diseases. These are mostly carried by aphids, so it is a good idea to spray the plants against them. A fungicide spray will also prevent the onset of botrytis and stem-rot moulds.

EVERGREEN HEDGES

Many gardeners, impatient with untidy evergreen hedges, prune them drastically in early to mid-spring and then learn to regret it. Depriving evergreens of their leaves gives them a check from which it takes them a long time to recover properly. Wait until this month, when, although still further growth will have taken place, it will be soft and easily clipped. A dense, well-furnished hedge will result, rather than a gappy, coarse one.

PRUNING CLEMATIS AND BROOM

Towards the end of the month, *Clematis montana* varieties will require pruning. They should only be pruned hard early in the year if they have become thoroughly out of hand, in which case you will have to sacrifice a year's flowers, as flowering takes place on the wood made in the previous year. Now that flowering is over, cut out the shoots on which the flowers were borne. This causes the plant to put all its energy into the growths that will flower next year. (For other Clematis see p.22).

Forms of the common broom (*Cytisus scoparius*) can be pruned back once they have flowered, and this applies to many of them this month, but take care not to cut into the old wood,as it has no growth buds. The only broom you can subject to 'renewal' pruning (severe cutting back to buds in the old wood) is the pineapple broom, *Cytisus battandieri*, which flowers at the end of this month and during next. The operation should be done after flowering and will induce new shoots from the base as well as from the buds. Check that the basal shoots are broom; many specimens are grafted onto laburnum, whose foliage is similar when young.

WALL SHRUBS AND CLIMBERS

As climbers and shrubs trained on walls grow, check them over and tie in the new growths as necessary, rubbing out surplus young shoots that are likely to grow away from the plane of the wall. Unfortunately they do not look at all good if you bend them round to tie them in and never grow properly.

MOWING THE LAWN

Modern thinking concerning mowing leads to the conclusion that it is better to leave the clippings on the lawn than to remove them. This depends on your point of view, as it presupposes frequent mowing in order to keep the clippings small. However, if you subscribe to the view that most lawns are overfed, yours will give rise to small clippings anyway, even if your mowing is not so frequent. The clippings will feed the lawn by being returned to it. Collected clippings are almost impossible to compost properly and make a very bad mulch, as they almost always contain weed seeds and attract moulds.

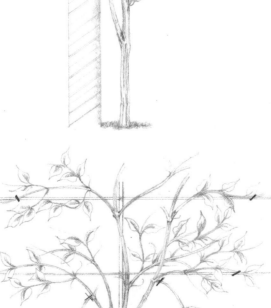

PLANTING

FUCHSIAS AND ANNUALS

I do not recommend planting shrubs and perennials during this and the next two months. If you can be sure to keep them watered and are not going away for longer than a short weekend, by all means plant anything irresistible that you find growing in a container. Other than that, restrict planting to half-hardy annuals and hardy fuchsias. The fuchsias should be planted with their crowns 5cm (2in) below soil level. This unusual practice is lethal to other shrubs but provides fuchsias with an opportunity to make strong, basal growths.

BLIND BULBS
Did you write down the week in which the last flowers faded on the bulbs you naturalised in grass? If you did, you should be in the qui vive for the seventh week thereafter, during which you can safely mow the grass. Do it earlier and the bulbs will come up blind (flowerless) next year.

DRIED DELPHINIUMS
You can enjoy delphiniums for months rather than weeks if you cut them, hang them in a dry, airy, cool shed in the dark, and then use the dried flowers in arrangements. They hold their colour better than most air-dried flowers.

EVERGREEN HEDGE PLANTS

Berberis (some)
Buxus (box)
Ilex (holly)
Lavender
Lonicera nitida
Privet
Pyracantha
Rhamnus
Taxus
Thuja

plants
OF THE
month
1

LUPIN
Russell Lupins

This race of multicoloured lupins must stand in the front rank of herbaceous perennials. Along with delphiniums and oriental poppies, they are the mainstay of early colour in the border, with aquilegias and the euphorbias that started last month acting as support. Russell lupins have recently been so improved upon as regards health, vigour, brightness of colour and ease of raising from seed that the modern strains can be regarded almost as a new race of plants.

type	Herbaceous perennials
flowers	Dense spikes in many colours, including bicolours
foliage	Deeply cut into 'fingers'; rich green
height	90cm–1.2m (3–4ft)
spread	60cm (2ft)
hardiness	Hardy
planting	Plant seed-raised plants, as those raised from cuttings may be infected with virus. Modern seed strains come almost true to colour
position	Plant among other herbaceous plants so that the spikes emerge from among them. Early-flowering perennials should always have later ones in front of them
soil	A good, well-manured border soil
propagation	From seed sown in a garden frame in early spring. Soak in tepid water for 24 hours before sowing
varieties	Choose modern seed strains, either mixed, such as 'Band of Nobles' or single colours or bicolours

▼ RODGERSIA
Rodgersia podophylla

Rodgersias are shade-loving plants that prefer ample moisture. They are primarily grown for their large, dramatic leaves, which in some species have a metallic-bronze finish that is most attractive. The feathery flowerheads, though not always freely borne, strike a bold note on an early summer's day.

type	Herbaceous perennial
flowers	Feathery heads of white
foliage	The finest in the genus. Large leaves have deep, irregular lobes that give them a jagged appearance. They are bronze when young, becoming green
height	90cm (3ft)

RODGERSIA PODOPHYLLA

spread	1.2m (4ft)
hardiness	Hardy
planting	Plant open-ground rodgersias in autumn. Container-grown plants are best planted in early spring or autumn
position	Part shade
soil	Moist but well-drained, leafy soil
propagation	By division in early spring, re-planting the divisions immediately into their final positions
alternatives	*R. pinnata* has large, pinnate leaves with bronze burnishing and pink flowers. *R. aesculifolia* is the best species for flowers, which may be white or creamy pink

MAGNOLIA
Magnolia wilsonii

It is often forgotten that the magnolias of spring are by no means the only ones. The summer magnolias differ in that they tend to produce a few flowers at a time over a long period, rather than having one enormous flush of bloom, but they make up for it by the delicacy and charm of the individual flowers.

type	Large deciduous shrub
flowers	Pendulous, white with crimson stamens
foliage	Typical magnolia paddle-shaped leaves
height	2.5m (9ft) after 10 years
spread	2m (7ft) after 10 years
hardiness	Vulnerable to severe frosts in late spring
planting	Best planted in late spring
position	Part shade
soil	Reasonably lime-tolerant. Prefers a soil to which organic matter has been added
pruning	None
propagation	By air layers or by semi-ripe cuttings taken in late summer and rooted under mist

HEMEROCALLIS 'ALAN'

DAY LILY
Hemerocallis Varieties

The day lilies are among the most accommodating of all garden plants. They will grow in almost all conditions and soils, stand up to competition, flower over a long season, propagate easily, provide a wide palette of colours – and yet are not nearly as widely grown as they deserve.

type	Herbaceous perennials
flowers	Large, lily-like, in all colours but blue, mauve and purple
foliage	Iris-like, but not stiff
height	Varies from 30 90cm (1 3ft)
spread	Clump-forming, 30–90cm (1–3ft)
hardiness	Hardy
planting	Plant in spring or autumn
position	Any apart from deep shade
soil	Any reasonable soil
propagation	By division just after the foliage starts to emerge – usually early spring. However, try to avoid disturbing the clumps until flowering starts to decline. This usually takes several years
alternatives	Lilies are far less easy than hemerocallis and often much less rewarding, but should nevertheless be attempted, especially those with scent, which is the one important quality almost entirely lacking in day lilies

tasks

FOR THE

month

2

**PLANTS FOR SIMPLE
LAYERING**

The great majority of woody plants
can be layered. Layering is
especially important in the
following genera, which are
difficult to propagate by other
means:

Calycanthus
Chionanthus
Cornus
Hamamelis
Kalmia
Magnolia
Paeonia (tree peonies)
Photinia
Rhododendron (including
deciduous azaleas)
Stachyurus
Stewartia

CHECKLIST

☐ Make layers of appropriate woody plants
☐ Thin early spring-sown hardy annuals to
15–20cm (6–8in) apart
☐ Survey your garden for areas of sun and shade

PROPAGATION

LAYERING

Layering is a propagation
technique in which the shoot
to be propagated is rooted
while still part of the parent
plant, and is not separated
from it until rooting is well
advanced.

It is a slow but reliable
method of propagation for
quite a wide range of plants,
most of them woody. It is
often regarded as crude, to
be scorned by those who are
good at taking cuttings, but
that is a mistaken viewpoint.
Layering is the method of
choice for certain shrubs,
among them deciduous
azaleas, magnolias and
many rhododendrons, that
are not easy otherwise
without specialised
equipment. It should be
noted, however, that a full
two years may elapse before
they are likely to have
rooted.

Simple layering

Simple layering is only
possible (1) if a branch can
be brought towards the
ground, or (2) if it can be
brought sufficiently low for a
pot of soil to be brought into
contact with it.

■ *Method 1*
Let us take *Magnolia* ×
soulangeana as an example.
It and the many magnolias
that share its general habit
regularly have branches that
sweep near to the ground,
ideal for simple layering.

■ Gently draw one such
branch down to the ground,
until the middle of one of its
new shoots touches the soil.
Label the shoot and let it go,
having marked the point on
the ground.

■ Dig the soil over to loosen
it and reduce it to the
consistency of a seedbed
after firming with the heels
(the soil should be just moist,
neither too dry nor too wet).
If it is light, add some peat
or leaf mould; if too heavy,
add the organic matter but
also work in a bucketful of
sand.

■ Go back to the shoot and,
at the point where it touched
the soil, make a diagonal slit
in its underside in the
direction of the tip and about
one third through the shoot.

■ Make a hole at the layering
point in the soil and bend

---

the shoot down into the
hole, so that it is comfortably
curved but not under strain.

■ Peg the shoot in position
with a wire hoop and then
fill the hole with soil, firming
it down afterwards. The tip
of the stem, with its foliage,
should be left pointing
upwards, as nearly vertically
as possible.

■ If there is strain on the
branch of which the layer is
part, drive a tent peg in
beneath it and guy the branch
down, but do not allow such
strain that the branch is
damaged.

NOTE

■ *This is the perfect month
for initiating layers. The
great majority of woody
plants are growing fast,
and the new tissues have
not yet become brittle. They
are also well charged with
the growth hormones that
allow them to make roots
adventitiously – that is to
say, on parts of the plants
where roots do not nor-
mally grow* ■

Transplanting

The layer will root over the next year or so, and you should plan to leave it undisturbed until the autumn of the year after it was layered, or even until the spring after that. However, if signs of strong growth are seen early next summer, sever the connection to the parent plant as a preparation

■ *Method 2*
With this method, a pot of soil is used instead of a hole in the ground for subjects without a branch that can be brought sufficiently far down. The pot is raised on suitable supports and the layer pegged into it. There is no difference in principle from method 1. It is most useful for layering *Camellia reticulata* varieties, which are very difficult indeed from cuttings.

for transplanting. It is never wise to separate the new plant and transplant it in the same operation.

Serpentine Layering

Plants with long, whippy stems can provide more than one layer from a branch.

■ Take branches of the current year's growth and peg them down at intervals, choosing leaf joints as the lowest points on the serpent.

■ Remove the leaves on these joints and make a slanting cut just below the joints before burying them.

■ As the angle of curve is not as great as in simple layering, it is often a good idea to prop each slit open with a pebble. Stems *will* root without wounding but they take a good deal longer and are not as certain.

PLANNING

●

SUN AND SHADE

You constantly read about the requirements of plants for shade, part shade, or full sun. Note that the expression 'part sun' is never used – I am unsure why not. Part shade is of two kinds: full shade for part of the day, such as that cast by buildings or dense shrubs, and the dappled shade provided by overhead trees. There is also a third, which is more theoretical but nonetheless important. 'Equivalent shade' is an expression of the sun's strength in different regions. Plants that need part or even full shade in warmer areas may need full sun where the climate is cooler. (It is worth noting in passing that almost all gardening operations on the North American continent are carried out at latitudes lower than those of the British Isles and that summer shade may be needed in America where none is necessary in Britain.)

It is not easy to estimate the sun and shade characteristics of the garden when you are planning your garden at the traditional time – midwinter. Neither can you be remotely precise at the main planting times – spring and autumn. It is now, when the sun is hot and high in the sky, that you should note carefully the places that are in full shade, shade for part of the day (and which part), and dappled shade.

PLANTS FOR SERPENTINE LAYERING

Clematis
Hedera
Jasmine
Vitis
Wisteria

plants
OF THE
month
2

HOSTA
Hosta 'Thomas Hogg'

Hostas are above all foliage plants. Their leaves are so variable in size and colour, and their habit so neat and ground-covering, that they are more in demand than almost any other border plants. It is not generally realised that, with the exception of those with white or cream variegation and just a few others, they are sun-tolerant when in a rich, organic, moisture-retentive soil. Many hostas are first-class flowering plants.

type	Herbaceous perennial
flowers	Like spikes of small, lilac lilies. This variety is one of the earliest to flower
foliage	Dark green with glossy undersides and broad, cream margins
height	60cm (2ft)
spread	50cm (20in)
hardiness	Hardy
planting	Plant at any time if from containers; autumn is best for bare-rooted plants
position	Part shade
soil	The richer and more organic the better. Lime-tolerant
propagation	By division in autumn or spring
alternatives	There are many variegated hostas, but few flower as prolifically or as early
special comment	Hostas are martyrs to slugs, so precautions should be taken or bait laid against them

ROSA 'EYEPAINT'

ROSE
Rosa 'Eyepaint'

Rose categories are not as definitely separated as is usually thought. Some old-fashioned roses, especially the Hybrid Perpetuals, closely resemble Hybrid Teas and some modern bush roses can perform the function of shrub roses in a garden.

type	Cluster-flowered (Floribunda) rose. Generally agreed to be more realistically thought of as a shrub rose. Unnamed seedling × 'Picasso'. McGredy, 1976
flowers	Large clusters of small, scarlet, white-eyed, single flowers with white reverses
habit and foliage	Like a shrub rose: very vigorous, strongly branching, bushy
height	Tall
spread	Wide-spreading
hardiness	Hardy
planting	Usually planted bare-rooted in winter, anytime if pot grown
position	Prefers full sun
soil	Well manured, tolerant of poorer soils than other floribundas
pruning	Shorten back long branches in autumn, then prune for shape in early spring. Do not prune hard
propagation	By budding
alternatives	Modern shrub roses such as 'Nevada' and 'Marguerite Hilling'
special comment	Prone to blackspot: spray regularly from early spring onwards

ROSE
Rosa 'Ruby Wedding'

This is the month during which the roses begin their summer-long display after the start provided by some early ones. The Large-Flowered (Hybrid Tea) roses are the mainstay of the rose garden.

type	Large-flowered (HT) bush rose. 'Mayflower' × unnamed seedling. Gregory, 1979
flowers	Crimson. Medium double, not full. Slight scent
habit and foliage	Short, bushy growth, medium-green foliage
height	Medium
spread	Medium
hardiness	Hardy
planting	Usually planted bare-rooted in winter but may be planted anytime from containers
position	Prefers full sun
soil	Well manured, on the heavy side, not too acid
pruning	Prune hard in early spring to outward-pointing buds
propagation	By budding
alternatives	Few combine its outstanding qualities
special comment	One of the very best roses for floristry, having few thorns, well-shaped blooms, and lasting well in water

ROSE
Rosa 'Intrigue'

After the start initiated by some early-flowered roses, now is when the rest begin their summer-long display. Along with the large-flowered (Hybrid Tea), the Cluster-flowered are the mainstay of the garden.

type	Cluster-flowered (Floribunda) rose. 'Grüss an Bayern' × unnamed seedling. Kordes, 1979
flowers	Many blooms to a cluster, very dark red. No scent
habit and foliage	Bushy growth, mid-green foliage
height	Medium
spread	Medium
hardiness	Hardy
planting	Usually planted bare-rooted in winter but may be planted anytime from containers
position	Prefers full sun
soil	Well manured, on the heavy side,

NYMPHAEA 'ESCARBOUCLE'

	not too acid
pruning	Hard pruning for exhibition blooms; otherwise fairly light for quantity of flower
propagation	By budding
alternatives	There are few floribunda roses with this luxuriantly deep colour

WATER-LILY
Nymphaea 'Escarboucle'

Water-lilies have been immensely popular since the Marliac nursery, in south-western France, discovered how to breed and develop hybrids during the second half of the nineteenth century.

type	Hybrid water-lily
flowers	Medium-sized, good red
foliage	Floating leaves, purple, turning to dark green
spread	1–1.3sq m (1–1½sq yd) (small to medium)
hardiness	Hardy
planting	Plant water-lilies in late spring
position	In sun. Do not plant near turbulent water, outlets of watercourses or fountains
soil	Plant in good, heavy soil, topped off with gravel. Do not use artificial fertilisers or fresh manure
propagation	By division in late spring, discarding the old, tough, main root and replanting the younger parts of the rhizome
alternatives	Other red lilies – 'Attraction' (medium-sized plant), 'Conqueror' (strong grower), 'Laydekeri' (miniature), 'Froebeli' (small)

practical project

A GREENHOUSE PROPAGATION UNIT

DIFFICULT CUTTINGS MADE EASIER BY MIST

Actinidia
Berberidopsis
Camellia
Campsis
conifers
Fothergilla
Ilex (holly)
Leptospermum
Lithodora
Magnolia
Parthenocissus
Rhododendron (including Azalea)
Sarcococca
Syringa (lilac)
Wisteria

How you make the best use of your greenhouse is largely a matter of personal priorities, but one thing is certain – greenhouses are not cheap and you should try to find ways of using yours to your utmost advantage.

Many people buy greenhouses and then find that their gardening interests change and that they no longer want to grow dozens of fuchsias and scores of 'geraniums'. They may also find that growing a variety of vegetables under glass has several snags, and that it is far from economical to devote the house just to one crop.

If your main interest is in the ornamental side of outdoor gardening, you are among the majority of gardeners, and if you have developed an interest in propagating, you are following the path down which all the best gardeners have passed. You are just the sort of person for whom the development of the greenhouse, or at least part of it, as a propagation unit is the ideal course of action.

There are several ways of organising such a unit but, again keeping an eye on the most advantageous use of the greenhouse, two main components are likely to take priority: a mist unit, for cuttings of the more difficult woody plants, and one or more heated frames for raising difficult seeds.

As space is at a premium, the greatest possible flexibility is wise, so the frames will be removable and can be stored when not needed.

THE MIST UNIT

A mist propagation unit consists of one or more atomising jets that play on the cuttings on the open bench. They are controlled by a device called an 'electronic leaf', which detects the level of moisture or operates on a time interval. The advantages of the system are:

- Cuttings can be rooted that are difficult or impossible by other methods
- Rooting is quicker and more certain
- Cuttings can be taken earlier and later
- Handling and management are made easier
- Wilting and scorching are greatly lessened
- There is much less need for shading, so more light can reach the cuttings. This and the above factor make for rapid root growth

You will need a mains electricity supply and mains water at no less than 25lb/sq in. You can buy kits, but it is cheaper to make your own system.

Staging
■ Firstly, make sure the staging is very strong, and if it is not, build it anew so that it can take the weight of 7.5cm (3in) depth of wet sand and a full load of seed trays and their compost. It should have a board rail all the way round no less than 10cm (4in) deep.

■ The base should be strong, and perforated at

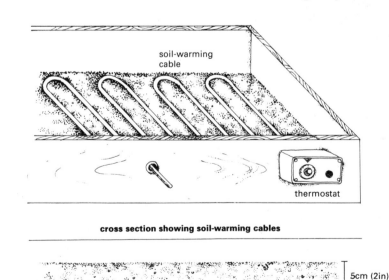

soil-warming cable

thermostat

cross section showing soil-warming cables

5cm (2in)

2.5cm (1in)

staging base

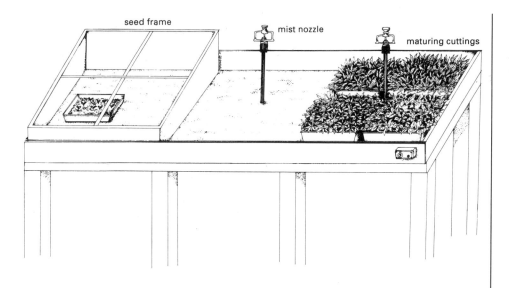

seed frame   mist nozzle   maturing cuttings

intervals with holes for drainage. It is not satisfactory to lay sheet plastic over wooden slats,
but stiff, corrugated plastic will do very well.

Heating
Bottom heat is essential.

■ Lay in a soil-warming cable, using the length
prescribed by the makers for the base area of
your unit. The cable will be laid on a bed of
sand 2.5cm (1in) deep in a series of loops.

WARNING

■ You must *use all the cable – it is dangerous
to attempt to shorten it ■*

■ The cable is controlled by a thermostat. The
optimum temperature is a constant 18–21°C
(65–70°F). The cable is eventually covered
with a further 5cm (2in) of sand.

■ A water pipe, running under the staging
base, branches at intervals at right angles so
that a branch is led up through the base to
terminate about 45cm (18in) above the sand in
a mist nozzle, consisting of a small aperture
through which the stream of water impinges on
a striker plate which atomises it. The nozzle is
adjustable.

■ The water is controlled by a solenoid valve in
the water line, which in its turn is controlled by
the electronic leaf, of which there are several
different types.

SEED FRAMES

Using a separate soil cable and thermostat, a
further length of staging can be converted into
bottom-heated frames for germinating seed.
They will greatly extend your seed-sowing
season and enable you to start sowing in late
winter – particularly important for trees and
shrubs, which need as long as possible in their
first year to become established. Your rates of
germination will be greatly increased, and you
will be able to obtain early germination of
dormant seed that has had to be chilled
beforehand.

■ If you are capable of making a cold frame
for outdoor purposes, you will have not the
slightest difficulty in making one or more
seed frames. Two are better than one, as you
can then move the pots from a tightly closed
one to another that is slightly open as the
seeds germinate, before taking them out
onto the open bench.

■ While germination is taking place, the frames
are best lightly shaded with material of no
greater density than muslin.

■ If you wish to use the space taken up by the
frame for other purposes, there is no problem
with making it removable, as it can simply rest
on the sand bed and inside the rails of the unit.
Because it does not have to stand up to
weather, it can be of relatively light construc-
tion, and clear plastic can be used instead of
glass.

A TIMELY TIP
*Next month sees the start of the
season for semi-ripe shrub
cuttings. They are the ones that
will benefit most from your mist
system, so try to have it up and
running by the end of this month
so that you can monitor the
characteristics of the electronic
leaf and check the general
running of the system before
taking any cuttings. When it is
running well without any pots of
cuttings, the sand should be
moistened at each firing of the
leaf but should just begin to dry
before the next. Adjust as
necessary when cuttings are
present. They should be
constantly coated with moisture
but the system should not create
general wetness.*

plant
selections

HERBACEOUS PERENNIALS

During the midsummer month (which by any standards is really its first one), herbaceous **peonies** enjoy the peak of their season – the earliest bloom at the end of spring; the latest in high summer.

They are not as widely grown as one might expect, largely due to a lack of understanding of their needs, but also because they are thought to contribute little outside their flowering period. This latter idea is hardly based on reality, as the pink or deep maroon shoots of newly emerged peonies are superb counterpoint to the narcissi of mid-spring.

To succeed with herbaceous peonies the crowns should be planted between 2.5–5cm (1–2in) inches below soil level. Any more inhibits flowering. They prefer a heavy soil to a light one, but take to acid and alkaline soils with equal aplomb. They are happy almost anywhere apart from deep shade, tolerate competition, and flower for half a century with just about no attention whatever.

Peonies have a palette restricted to the red tones of the spectrum and to white, but that allows for all kinds and combinations of pink, rich purple shades, and startling whites, as well as flamboyant, clean reds. The flower shapes – single, double and Imperial (semi-double, in which the centres of the flowers are filled with petaloid stamens) – allow for permutations of colour and flower style that provide a very wide choice of varieties.

Hemerocallis, known as day lilies for their extremely long succession of flowers that individually last but a day, have much in common with peonies. They, too, are less widely grown than they deserve, and they show an even greater toleration of widely differing growing conditions.

Day lilies can grow perfectly happily in the wettest, boggiest conditions and can thrive lustily on the driest, sunniest bank. They can live as isolated specimens, in large, jostling drifts, or even in grass, and soil content is of small concern to them. Just as with peonies, long-term neglect suits them well, and they should only be moved or divided when flowering starts to fall off, which is usually only after many years.

Their colour range is wider than that of peonies. They are, of course, a totally different style of plant, with iris-like leaves and lily-like flowers; resemblances are limited to their generally easy-going natures. Reds tend to a brick tone, but there are some fine, clear scarlets and deep crimsons, while the yellows are cool and clean or warm and rich. There are peach, apricot, salmon, mahogany, and many shades of pink, but blues, lilacs and lavenders are absent.

The ineffable blues of **delphiniums** are one of early summer's glories. Unfortunately, far too many seed-raised plants are seen whose colours are muddied by brownish purple. Named varieties – 'Loch Leven', 'Blue Nile', 'Cristella' and others – provide a purity of blue that is seldom seen in plants other than these and **Meconopsis**, the blue poppies of the Himalayas that start into stately flower in the peatier parts of the garden this month.

Against these and the gentler oriental poppies (some of the orange ones are just too strident), the flat heads of **achilleas** strike a different colour note as well as lending a difference of texture to the bed with their flat heads all of a plane. The contrast with the upright spikes of delphiniums and lupins is most marked. However, there is a coarseness about them that demands that they be used with discretion, but the clearest of the yellow varieties have great value.

A BORDER ACHILLEA

The **diascia** season – a long one, lasting well into early autumn – starts this month. This is a genus that is virtually new to gardens. In the early 1970s there was but one hardy species and no varieties; now South Africa and the hybridists (of whom your author was the first) have yielded up about another thirty.

Their nemesia-like flowers, almost always in some shade of clear, soft pink, are unlike anything else among perennials. They have a special value when set at the front of a border, keeping it continuously colourful right through the parade of arrivals and departures in the taller ranks. Try very soft cuttings (see p.122). They root easily as long as you pinch the tops out, even before they have rooted.

to the later, high summer. So it is just right that **philadelphus**, the scented, white mock orange in all its guises – single, double, small and large – should be at its best just now. It does little for the rest of the year, but this is a month of rest from flowering for the shrub world as a whole, and the fairly nondescript bushes earn their keep.

Deutzias, again mostly white, although some are lilac, enjoy their fleeting moment of glory this month. There are still some **late rhododendrons** about, although a hot spell will shorten their show, and **weigelas**, some **lilacs** and a few **viburnums** continue to play their part. **Clematis** and **jasmines** are needed now, and **wisterias** glorify it.

ROSES AND SHRUBS

Repeat-flowering roses, too, set out on their long flowering season. Of the Hybrid Teas and Floribundas there is little ignorance – everyone knows a rose when they see one – but shrub roses are neglected in favour of their more glamorous cousins. There is these days a wide selection, and a well thought-out choice of just a few makes a fine framework around which the other roses can congregate.

This is a soft, 'cottagey' month in the garden, one where light scents, delicate colours and simplicity rule. The more regal, sophisticated, evening sorts of effects are appropriate

ALPINES

On the rock garden, little **cranesbills** (the true geraniums), alpine **hypericums**, and shrubby **penstemons** lead the field. It is hard not to love the cranesbills, especially such gems as *Geranium sanguineum lancastriense* (now *G.s. – striatum*), whose softest pink, darker-veined flowers come from just one sandy island close to the coast of northern England – Walney Island, and 'Ballerina', a man-made hybrid whose dark purple veining on lilac just, but only just, stays short of a sophistication that would disqualify it from a home in what is essentially the domain of wildings.

DELPHINIUMS AND LUPINS

plants

IN

flower

KEY

* = evergreen   spp = species
vars = varieties

NOTES

Daboecia cantabrica requires lime-free peaty soil. *Magnolia sieboldii* and *Kalmia latifolia* need lime-free soil.
B. globosa is hardy in southern areas.
Cistus do well in hot dry spots and *Escallonia* vars are good for coastal districts.

FUCHSIA FORMALITY

If you like formal bedding schemes using fuchsias, try standards in varieties whose flowers are in the pink, red or white range with little or no purple, and set them among light pink petunias. The petunias should have been chosen or sown specially for the purpose. A strain such as 'Super Cascade Blush', an improved F₁ hybrid that comes true to colour, is ideal. Edge the bed with *Senecio bicolor cineraria* (syn. *Cineraria maritima, Senecio cineraria*), whose felt-white leaves emphasise the silvery effect you will have achieved, even though the motif colour is pink. This scheme will stay in full decorative order until the frosts, and all you have to do is weed it and keep it tidy.

TREES	colour	flower type
Liriodendron tulipifera	Greenish yellow	Like tulips
Robinia pseudoacacia several vars	White	Pea shaped
Styrax japonica	White	Like snowdrops; all along undersides of branches
SHRUBS		
Berberis deciduous vars	Yellow	
Buddleia globosa (Orange ball tree)	Orange	
*Carpenteria californica	White	Large, flat
*Cistus spp and vars	Various	5–10cm (2–4in) wide
*Convolvulus cneorum	White	Typical of convolvulus
Cornus kousa chinensis	White	Bracts
Cytisus spp and vars (Broom)	Various	Pea shaped
*Daboecia cantabrica	Purplish red or white	Heather-like
Daphne 'Somerset'	Mauve-pink	Clusters, scented
Deutzia spp and vars	White; some are lilac-pink	Bell shaped
*Escallonia vars	White, pink or red	Small, bell shaped
*Hebe many	White, red or purple	Spikes
*Helianthemum vars	Various	
*Hypericum 'Hidcote'	Yellow	Large, round
*Kalmia latifolia	Soft rose	Small, clustered
Magnolia sieboldii	White	Chalices
Philadelphus vars	Mostly white	Scented
Potentilla fruticosa vars	Various	Dog-rose shaped
*Prunus lusitanica (Portuguese laurel)	White	Plumes
*Rhododendron the hardy hybrids	Various	
Rosa many	Various	
Viburnum opulus	White	Flat heads
'Sterile'	White	Round heads
Weigela vars	Pink, white or red	Foxglove-like
CLIMBERS	**colour**	**flower type**
Clematis large flowered	Various	
Jasmine hardy types	White	Scented
Lonicera (Honeysuckle)	Yellow and pink	Scented
Wisteria vars	Lilac, white, purple or rose	Scented

PERENNIALS

PERENNIALS	colour	height
Achillea spp and vars	White, yellow	60–90cm (24–36in)
'Galaxy Hybrids'	Cream, buff or pink	45–60cm (18–24in)
Alstroemeria	Various, including yellow and orange	60cm (24in)
Astilbe vars	Red, pink or white	60cm (24in)
Astrantia major	White, tinged green	60cm (24in)
Campanula lactiflora	Blue or white	1.2m (48in)
latifolia	Blue or white	1.2m (48in)
persicifolia	Shades of blue	90cm (36in)
Centaurea dealbata	Pink	60cm (24in)
Centranthus ruber	Pink, red or white	80cm (32in)
Coreopsis vars	Yellow	60–75cm (24–30in)
Delphinium vars	Blue, mauve, purple or white, tall spikes	1.2–1.5m (4–5ft)
Dianthus many vars	Variations of pink	20–40cm (8–16in)
Eremurus bungei	Yellow spikes in orange	1.5m (5ft)
Geranium endressii vars	Pink, veined	30cm (12in)
'Russell Pritchard'	Magenta pink	30cm (12in)
Hemerocallis vars	Various	30–60cm (12–24in)
Heuchera vars	Pink or white	30–45cm (12–18in)
Iris germanica (Bearded iris)	Various	75–100cm (30–40in)
Leucanthemum × superbum vars	White	45–80cm (18–32in)
Lysimachia punctata	Yellow	75cm (30in)
Oenothera missouriensis	Large, lemon yellow	20cm (8in)
Paeonia herbaceous vars	Red, pink, white	75cm (30in)
Papaver orientale	Red, pink, orange or white	75cm (30in)
Primula candelabra and bog spp	Various	45–90cm (18–36in)
Trollius spp and vars	Orange or yellow	45–60cm (18–24in)
Verbascum vars	Yellow or pink	1m (40in)

BULBS

BULBS	colour	height
Allium vars (Ornamental onion)	Various	20–45cm (8–18in)
Camassia spp	Blue or cream	30–70cm (12–28in)
Iris Pacific Coast Hybrids	Yellow or purple	45cm (18in)
English vars	Blue, purple or white	60cm (24in)
Lilium martagon vars	Purple or white	90cm (36in)

EVENING ANNUALS

Nictotianas, stocks and mignonette are among the scented annuals that no garden should be without. There is nothing more pleasant than that first time when the perfume of evening annuals reaches you as you settle down for a pre-dinner drink on the terrace. You will experience it many times during the summer, but the magic is never quite as complete again.

ROCK GARDEN

Achillea spp
***Androsace sarmentosa** vars
Aster alpinus
Campanula spp
***Dianthus** spp and vars
***Edraianthus** spp
Erigeron spp
Erodium spp
***Geranium** spp
***Gypsophila repens**
***Helianthemum** vars
Hypericum spp
***Leontopodium alpinum** (edelweiss)
Linum spp
***Penstemon** spp
***Phlox** spp and vars
***Sedum** spp
***Thymus serpyllum** and vars
Veronica spp

JULY

I should like to enjoy this summer flower by flower . . .
ANDRE GIDE

Among shrubs at any rate, early summer is like half-time in a football match. Those that bloom in spring on the wood made the previous year are separated from those that flower in high summer on the wood of the current year by an interval, during which a show is put on to keep our attention. The break over, summer swings into action.

It is the peak of the year for herbaceous perennials. They clamour for the attention of pollinating insects and it is all too easy to have planted them so that they are all clamour and far too little harmony. This is a month during which lack of planning becomes all too apparent and results in many a wince as magenta screams at scarlet and dark crimson argues bitterly with light purple.

We may scoff at those who meticulously draw up plans on paper for their plantings. Indeed, some inspired gardeners seem to manage beautifully on instinct and ad hoc *associations. But the wise person knows how short memory is and that foresight is the key to consistent success. When you see* Lychnis coronaria *'Atrosanguinea' in a public garden, planted against neutral green, and then try to recall its colour at planting time in autumn, are you likely to remember that it was tooth-gratingly magenta, or will your memory, full of thoughts of a lovely day out, recall it as rich red? Again, the value of an active notebook is evident.*

This is a somnolent month, but the solstice is past, the first signs of the decline of the year are just discernible, and as you enjoy the comfort of the summer weather you will feel, if you are truly attuned to nature, the stirrings of a primeval imperative. For our ancestors complacency was lethal; there was much to do to ensure survival during the cold to come. That is why, in midsummer, gardeners sit up suddenly and say, 'Can't sit here all day, you know. There's lots to be done'.

AUGUST

August creates as she slumbers,
replete and satisfied.

JOSEPH WOOD KRUTCH

*Whereas last month summer reached its fulfilment, now is a time
of transition. To begin with, colour and form seem held in a stasis
of time, and little changes. Colours are true and sometimes fierce:
reds flame purely, blues glow coolly, and green is as green can be.
Then, towards the month's end, a weariness can be seen to have
crept in. There is a hint of russet in the reds, a bleaching of
yellows, and blues show their age by a muddying of purple.
Among the greens, the keynotes of the garden since the spring
began, the golden buff of straw heralds the onset of autumn.
How you react to these changes depends on your personality, your
mood, and your view of the horticultural year. A pessimist, or
one who sees the year linearly, can hardly bear to part with
summer's glory. Someone for whom the year is an expression of
circular time, however, will find himself able to look forward to
autumn cyclamen, fall foliage colour, and even beyond, to
snowdrops in the spring.
Isolated thus from the bustling past and the running down of the
year that is to come, this month has much to offer in the well-
planned garden. To those who think in seasons, rather than
months, it is too easily lost between 'summer' and 'autumn' and
allowed no character of its own. Yet it can be the most individual
of months, redolent of all the quiet satisfaction that goes with an
unaccustomed afternoon nap taken while on holiday.
There are many plants which are now at their flowering peak, but
many more that have carried on from earlier in the summer or
even, in some cases, from late spring. They all join together in a
last glorious crescendo of richness and colour before the quiet
melody of autumn gently takes over.*

plant
selections

Hydrangea aspera is one of the most natural-looking species and grows happily in part shade

SHRUBS

Calluna vulgaris, the **common heather**, is only 'common' on moorland in western Europe, a sliver or two of North Africa, and Iceland. It arrived in Nova Scotia as seeds on the heather used by settlers as packing for their belongings, and has spread to gardens everywhere in the temperate world.

It is one of the glories of late summer and continues to make a magnificent contribution all the way through to late autumn, when the last few varieties flower. When varieties are selected with foliage ranging through many shades of green, grey-green, grey, silver, gold and russet, heather can play a year-round part in the garden with which very little else can compete.

Clematis of the kind that need to be cut back every early spring to within 30cm (1ft) of the ground look wonderful when growing over the heathers, but need to be chosen with care lest their colours, manifest at the same time of year, should clash. Clear red (such as the texensis clematis 'Gravetye Beauty') or a fairly pure blue ('Elsa Späth') will enhance, rather than quarrel with the heather flowers.

Possibly because of a loss of the identity of this month in the general concept of 'summer', some of its own particular treasures are all too often overlooked and can even acquire unjustified reputations for difficulty, merely because they are seldom seen. **Eucryphias** are a case in point – superb evergreen shrubs with crops of white flowers of a ravishing purity set against deep, almost black-green leaves.

They are thought of as being on the tender side, yet most are anything but. I have seen *Eucryphia* 'Nymansay' flourishing and flowering beautifully in some of the coldest parts of Britain, as well as in the mildest, kindest places in Ireland. It will, in time, grow tall, but no more than many slow-growing conifers, and clothes itself to ground level with small, stiff, prettily shaped leaves. Late summer sees large flowers, the white equivalent, if you like, of *Hypericum* 'Hidcote', equally coming down to the ground.

In Leicestershire, England, between which and Moscow there is not a single hill to break the howling viciousness of the east winds, the owner of a beautifully shaped 'Nymansay' told me that growing heathers right up to its 'skirts' gave it the coolness at the root as well as the protection from having its soil frozen that was the secret of its success.

Blue is always welcome, no more so than at this time of year, when delphiniums are a memory and the eye might just yearn for relief from the yellows and reds that are so typical of the month. Two small shrubs, for which the smallest garden surely has room, provide it for a few of the weeks of high summer.

Caryopteris × clandonensis is a rounded shrub not much more than 90cm (3ft) high, especially when given the preferred treatment, which is to cut it back quite hard in spring. This keeps it bushy and encourages it to make a dense mass of small, greyish, aromatic leaves and generously to produce its clusters of bright blue flowers. There are four or five different varieties, of which 'Arthur Simmonds' is marginally the best.

It shares a liking for dry soil in sun with the hardy plumbago, **Ceratostigma plumbaginoides.** This possessor of one of the more fearsome names among plants is again a 90cm (3ft) charmer. Its leaves are also small, but glossy, and its flowers are a little larger, just like those of plumbago, but almost royal blue.

Ceanothus are larger shrubs whose contribution to the presence of blue in the garden cannot be over-praised. There are species and varieties to grace every month from spring to early autumn, and the Delilianus group of ceanothus are especially to be sought after for

HERBACEOUS PERENNIALS

the high-summer period. *C.* × *delilianus* itself is a medium-sized, deciduous shrub with soft blue flowers all summer long, and the others are cast in the same mould. 'Gloire de Versailles' has large flower clusters that last until autumn, 'Henri Desfosse' is deep, violet blue, and 'Indigo' is, as you might imagine, even deeper in colour.

Yuccas are, like eucryphias, misunderstood. It is a fallacy to equate an exotic appearance with tenderness or difficulty of cultivation. Many yuccas are indomitably hardy, though their agave-like foliage, like so many outward-pointing swords, suggests the margins of deserts and scrub wherein coyotes might lie up by day. In fact, such a picture is not that inaccurate, as the south-eastern United States are their main area of distribution, but they are subject to hard frosts in nature and it is only the weight of snow that is likely to do much harm.

I do not suggest you try yuccas too far from the moderating effects of a maritime location or, failing that, shelter from the coldest winds, but I do suggest that they be grown more widely. Their enormous, white flowers in stately spikes are one of the special treats of the warmest part of the year.

Above all, it is perennials that dominate the late-summer scene. Those with long flowering seasons that started earlier in the summer are caught up by those whose proper season is just pre-autumn, and the combination leads to the richest time in the garden for concentrations of flower power. It is an awe-inspiring time, representing in cultivation the full, urgent thrust of botanical nature, as the plants call out for one last reproductive effort before their options close down.

THE YEAR'S CLIMAX

Add to all this the burgeoning of **annuals**, the continuing activity in the **water-lily** production line, the formation of elegant, golden flowerheads among **ornamental grasses**, the maturing of **hydrangeas** from cool misses into sumptuously-clad matrons, and then stop to think. How ever did you fail to realise that, if spring is when the flower garden year really starts, high summer is its climax?

Alchemilla mollis, *penstemons, lupins and astrantias, demonstrating that the late-summer border can look as interestingly fresh as any day in spring*

AUGUST
113

plants
IN
flower

KEY

* = evergreen   spp = species
vars = varieties

NOTES

Clethra alnifolia vars and **Berberidopsis corallina** require lime-free soil.
Berberidopsis is moderately hardy.
Lapageria rosea is on the tender side and should be grown in the shade.
Myrtus spp are not hardy in cold areas.

CONIFER AND HEATHER CLICHÉ

If you possibly can, try to avoid a plant association that is now utterly passé: the conifer-and-heather bed. Few plantings are quite as satisfying to lovers of natural-looking gardens than undulating carpets of heathers, and the summer heathers – particularly the host of varieties of *Calluna vulgaris* – make an overwhelmingly important contribution to the lime-free garden with their wide range of foliage colours, sizes, habits of growth and late summer flowers. A gnarled specimen of *Pinus sylvestris* 'Beuvronensis', never attaining more than 90cm (3ft) in height in a long life, is perfect among them, as are some of the dwarfer willows, trees that represent those you might reasonably expect to find on the moorland among the heathers. But geometrically conical spruces, tightly columnar junipers, and chamaecyparis like large bathroom sponges combine with heathers to create the ultimate in horticultural kitsch. Worse, after you have seen several such plantings all within the bounds of one suburb, they become boringly predictable.

SHRUBS	colour	flower type
Caryopteris × clandonensis	Blue	In neat heads
Ceanothus × delilianus and vars	Blue	Conical heads
Ceratostigma willmottianum	Blue	Like those of plumbago
Clerodendrum bungii	Purplish red	Heads like mophead hydrangeas
trichotomum fargesii	White, in maroon calyces	Very fragrant
Clethra alnifolia vars	White or pink	Small, in terminal clusters, sweet scent
Genista tinctoria	Yellow	Broom-like
Hibiscus syriacus vars	Various	Mallow-like
Indigofera spp	Pink or purplish rose	Pea shaped
*Itea ilicifolia	Greenish white	Long 'tassels'
Leycesteria formosa	White with purple bracts	Hanging clusters
*Myrtus spp (Myrtle)	White	Starry
Olearia spp	White	Daisies
*Yucca spp	White	Spires of large bells

Also: **Abelia, Buddleia, Colutea, Convolvulus cneorum, Cytisus, Desfontainea, Erica, Escallonia, Fuchsia, Hebe, Hydrangea, Hypericum, Lavandula, Ligustrum, Magnolia grandiflora, Perovskia, Phygelius, Potentilla, Romneya, Roses, Ruta, Spartium, Spiraea, Tamarix, Teucrium, Vinca**

CLIMBERS

	colour	flower type
Berberidopsis corallina	Crimson	Rounded, hanging from long stalks
Campsis 'Mme Galen'	Salmon-red	Large trumpets
Clematis many vars	Various	
Lapageria rosea	Rose	Large, waxy trumpets
Lonicera (Honeysuckle) late vars	Various	Fragrant
Mutisia oligodon	Salmon pink	Like gazanias
Pileostegia viburnoides	Creamy white	Hydrangea-like

PERENNIALS

Most of the perennials that flowered last month carry their peak of flowering over into this. The following are perennials that generally appear this month but *not* last. In their turn, many of them continue into early autumn.

	colour	height
Anaphalis triplinervis	White everlastings	45cm (18in)
Anchusa vars	Blue	90cm (36in)
Anemone × hybrida vars	Pink or white	1.5m (60in)

Catananche caerulea	Lavender blue or white	60cm (24in)
Cimicifuga racemosa	White	90cm (36in)
Galega × hartlandii	Lilac or lavender	1.5m (60in)
Limonium platyphyllum	Lavender or pink	30cm (12in)
Lobelia hybs	Bright red	90cm (36in)
Penstemon many	Shades of red, pink or white	75cm (30in)
Platycodon grandiflorum 'Mariesii'	Large blue bells	45cm (18in)
Polygonum spp	Crimson or pink	25–75cm (10–30in)
Rudbeckia spp and vars	Yellow or orange	60cm–1.3m (24–52in)
Salvia turkestanica	Bluish white with rose bracts	1.2m (48in)
Sedum spectabile and vars	Red or pink	45cm (18in)
Stokesia laevis	Blue	45cm (18in)
Tradescantia vars	Blue, white or rose	45cm (18in)
Zantedeschia aethiopica	White arum lily	60cm (24in)
Zauschneria californica (now *Epilobium canum*)	Scarlet	30cm (12in)

Also: **Achillea, Agapanthus, Anthemis, Astilbe, Astrantia, Campanula, Centaurea, Centranthus, Coreopsis, Crinum, Crocosmia, Dianthus, Dictamnus, Echinacea, Echinops, Eryngium, Geranium, Geum, Gypsophila, Helenium, Helianthus, Heliopsis, Hemerocallis, Heuchera, Hosta, Kniphofia, Leucanthemum superbum, Liatris, Ligularia, Lychnis, Lysimachia, Lythrum, Monarda, Nepeta, Oenothera, Phlox, Physostegia, Potentilla, Scabiosa, Sidalcea, Solidago, Thalictrum, Veronica.**

BULBS	colour	height
*Cyclamen europaeum	Pink, fragrant	10cm (4in)
Galtonia candicans	White, tinged green	1.2m (48in)
Nerine bowdenii	Pink	30cm (12in)

ROCK GARDEN

Ceratostigma plumbaginoides	*Geranium* spp
Crassula sarcocaulis	*Oenothera* spp
Cyclamen europaeum	*Polygonum* spp
Dianthus spp and vars	*Sedum* spp
Gentiana – Asiatic	*Silene schafta*
	Tunica saxifraga

LIVING ACCENTS

At a time when there is so much colour about, it is all too easy for the garden to take on an over-stuffed look, rather like a Victorian drawing room. It is a good idea to stand back and, with as objective an eye as you can muster, take stock of the structure of the garden. Is it standing up to the great surge of late summer colour? Or is it submerged by it?

If the answer to the first question is an honest affirmative, it probably means that you have got two important aspects of your garden design right: the balance of greenery and flowers, and the provision of accents. The former point hardly needs to be belaboured; the latter is one whose importance is all too often neglected.

Accents are easy to provide by using artefacts – fountains, gazebos of different kinds and even 'statuary' for which an entirely lamentable fashion has emerged in recent years. What is not so easy, and is far more rewarding, is to create accents using plants.

At this time of year, an illustration of this is easy to find. Yuccas, which are fairly conspicuous at all times, now become commanding features when they erupt in fountains of large, creamy bells. The tall spikes of flowers are the perfect complement to the clumps of sword-like leaves, and the plants are in tune with almost any style of garden, formal or informal, small or large.

ARTFUL TIDINESS

Towards the end of the month, deadheading becomes a necessity. It was an occasional obligation last month, something constantly at the edge of consciousness in the first weeks of this, but now it takes over as the key to the good appearance of the flower garden. No matter how carefully you have planned and planted for late-summer associations of flower colour and form, browned, distorted flowerheads will ruin your efforts as would curry stains on your best Ralph Lauren. This is really only the beginning. As next month progresses, you will find the job increasingly demanding and less and less restricted to flowers, until it culminates in the great autumn cut-back of perennials.

Nevertheless, keep an open eye for flowerheads that are not so much dead as extra-mature. Watch for the calyces left after flowers have dropped, the changing textures and colours of hydrangeas, and the interesting brown of the spent stems of astilbes. Be tidy, but avoid being too meticulous. You are aiming for your gardening to be artistic rather than twee, and you should be alert to beauty in whatever form it takes. There are a full six months of the true gardening year to come. Whoever coined the phrase 'putting the garden to bed', so often used as summer comes to a close, was indeed a philistine.

SEPTEMBER

Summer ends, and Autumn comes, and he who
would have it otherwise would have high tide
always and a full moon every night.

HAL BORLAND

*Last month in temperate latitudes was the throbbing height of
summer, but carried with it a tendency to create a desire for its
end. Guiltily, we begin to look forward to cooler conditions, to
soft rain and damper breezes. They may not come during the first
few days of this month, yet for some reason those days bring
sudden changes. The ranks of the great colour parade of past
weeks thin dramatically and new plants take the stage, but in
considerably fewer numbers.*

*As the month progresses, early autumn's mature palette casts a
veil of russets and dusky reds over the garden, enlivened here and
there by white and an occasional splash of old gold. The
background is still green, but a darker, more sombre, middle-aged
range of tones, flashed here and there with amber.*

*Towards the end, grandmotherly purples, mauves, and discreetly
understated reds enjoy a major celebration, but the equinox brings
the first gales, the soil softens rapidly under the first serious rains
of autumn, and the fireside begins to beckon. Suddenly, the
evenings are long again, and gardening books are taken from
shelves as plans are laid for future springs and summers.*

*But you have no urgency in that direction, have you? For you
have been planning all along. And because you know what this
time of year is capable of, you are by no means surprised when a
lower, but still hot sun persists in delivering strong and poignant
reminders of the summer just gone. That is when the month casts
its subtle spell; when stillness and warmth take over under the
rich, slanting light, and you join the bees and the last butterflies
among the theatrical flowers of autumn.*

tasks

FOR THE

month

1

CHECKLIST

- ☐ Clear paths of weeds
- ☐ Check your stocks of garden chemicals
- ☐ Prune rambler roses
- ☐ Transplant evergreen shrubs
- ☐ Plant spring-flowering bulbs
- ☐ Cut back dead and dying foliage in the pond, and stretch netting over the pond to catch falling leaves
- ☐ Clear tired annuals and compost them. Prepare windowboxes, tubs and beds for next month's planting of spring bedding
- ☐ In the herbaceous border, cut back seeding stems unless you wish to retain them for seed or flower arrangements
- ☐ Move tender perennials into the greenhouse before frost strikes
- ☐ Lift gladioli and sort out the old and new corms. Store the new ones in a frost-free shed

MAINTENANCE

CLEARING PATHS

The path weedkillers for which it is claimed that they keep all growth down for an entire season certainly do so, but it depends on what you mean by a 'season'. Applying one in spring will give you a full six months of weed-free paths and drives, but it is unrealistic to expect it to last for a whole year. Weed seeds are bound to have found their way into the cracks between paving or among the gravel during the summer, and you should give an application of weedkiller again now to give cover until next spring.

GARDEN CHEMICALS

A general word on chemicals. They are not evil substances to be avoided at all costs and are only deleterious if they escape into the environment as a result of being used to excess. Weedkillers, insecticides and fertilisers that are applied excessively find their way into the water supplies, kill flying insects, harm other wild life, and take up energy reserves in their manufacture.

Used sensibly and to an extent that ensures their efficacy but no more, they are essential tools in the preparation and maintenance of a good flower garden. Without them, all the organic cultivation in the world will not keep weeds to a level people in full-time work have time to control, nor will it counteract the unnatural concentrations of insect

The more effective of these agents combine pre-emergent with contact weedkillers. They are highly efficient, but spring applications will to a large extent have been leached away.

pests caused by the crop pattern of the countryside and townscapes.

Organic cultivation greatly assists the strength of plants and their ability to combat pests and diseases, but its definition does not exclude inorganic aids. In maintaining your ornamental garden, you can combine the generous use of organic materials with the judicious use of chemicals and leave the environment none the worse.

Care and disposal of chemicals

Where you *can* do untold damage is in the methods you use to get rid of surplus or unwanted chemicals. They must never, ever, be poured down drains. The advice sometimes given to dig a hole and pour surplus chemicals into it is unintelligent in the extreme. Firstly, buy discriminately and only in small quantities; secondly, contact your local authority if you have any you wish to dispose of, no matter how small the quantity.

WARNING

- *You should never use a pesticide in the year after it was bought. They nearly all deteriorate and weaken. If you spray pests with a weakened pesticide, the strongest will survive to breed, reinfest, and build up a resistant strain that will then travel to other gardens*

This month and next, see to your stocks of chemicals. Are they properly and safely stored? Do you really need all the ones you have? Is it not time you got rid of all the old stock? Contact the appropriate officer of your local authority and ask advice on disposal. Then think green, with the emphasis on the 'think'.

PRUNING RAMBLER ROSES

Now is the time to prune rambler roses. Do this by cutting back flowered stems and tying in the best of the current year's shoots.

THE POND

Cut back dead and dying foliage to prevent it decaying in the pond and fouling the water. Towards the end of the month, stretch netting over the pond to catch falling leaves – for the same reason. During thundery spells, increase the force of the jet from the garden hose by placing your thumb over the end, and spray the water surface to increase oxygenation.

PLANTING

TRANSPLANTING EVERGREENS

Early autumn is one of the times – late spring is the other – when evergreen shrubs that resent movement at other times of the year can be transplanted with the minimum of risk.

With some exceptions, evergreens are difficult to transplant successfully because they do not become dormant in the winter but carry on losing moisture from their leaves, moisture which has to be drawn from the soil by the roots. If the roots are damaged, as they almost always are in transplanting, there is bound to be stress on the plant.

From the middle of this month to the beginning of

next, the soil is warm enough for vigorous root growth to take place, and the air is cool enough to keep water loss down to an acceptable level. The colder your garden, the earlier you should move the shrubs. This does not apply to rhododendrons, azaleas, young camellias and most members of the heather family (Ericaceae), whose roots make fibrous mats that can be lifted in their entirety. They can be moved at any time of year except in extremes of weather. Hollies, laurels, and other evergreen shrubs with woodier, more wide-spreading root systems must be moved only during these narrow windows of opportunity.

Every effort should be made to dig out as much of the root system as possible intact and with the soil still attached. When replanting follow the method for planting shrubs on p.150.

Shrubs are moved for several reasons, but unfortunately the most usual one is because the initial planting was too crowded. The majority of gardeners – not the few – make the mistake of trying to fill their gardens too soon. If you are restrained when planting and allow shrubs to have room to grow properly you will save on pruning, combating disease and, eventually, the labour of transplanting.

SPRING-FLOWERING BULBS

This month is the time to plant spring-flowering bulbs. It is important to get them settled earlier rather than later, as they soon start to make roots. Tulips, however, can be planted next month so that they do not produce precocious shoots that are likely to be frosted.

TRANSPLANTING EVERGREEN SHRUBS

Dig a trench around the shrub – beyond the extent of its branches

Use a spade to cut under the root ball – dig out as much of the root system as possible

To make moving the shrub easier, a pole strapped to its base allows for lifting with an assistant

TOP TIPS FOR PLANTING BULBS

If you make the planting hole for each bulb three times the height of the bulb and make sure the bulb is sitting firmly on the bottom, the planting depth will be just right.

If you are thinking of naturalising bulbs in grass, plant them between one-and-a-half times and twice the normal depth. This will ensure that the inevitable compaction caused by foot traffic and mowers does not harm the bulbs.

For a more natural look to bulbs in grass, take a double handful of bulbs and throw them away from you. Plant each where it lands. Any that land so that they touch should be separated, but resist the temptation to be tidy. Plant any outliers just where they land – they will help create the illusion.

plants
OF THE
month
1

CHRYSANTHEMUM
Dendranthema 'Grandchild'

Chrysanthemum has been split by the botanists into several new genera, and the plants we have always known so well as 'chrysanths' now fall within the genus *Dendranthema* and include the Reflexed, Incurved, Intermediate and other classes. We have to learn new names, such as *Argyranthemum*, *Chrysanthemopsis*, and *Arctanthemum*, but *Dendranthema* is destined to become the most familiar.

type	Pompon chrysanthemum: semi-hardy herbaceous perennial
flowers	Small, button-like, pink, darker at centre
foliage	Small, neat
height	45cm (18in)
spread	30cm (1ft)
hardiness	Hardy in fairly mild areas. Elsewhere, lift and store during winter
planting	Best planted in spring. Planting should be shallow
position	Full sun
soil	A good, fertile, well-manured border soil
propagation	Take cuttings 5cm (2in) long in spring
alternatives	'Mei Kyo' (purple and pink), 'Mavis' (similar to 'Grandchild' but lighter colour), 'Golden Treasure' (orange-gold), 'Imp' (crimson)

DENDRANTHEMA 'GRANDCHILD'

JAPANESE ANEMONE
Anemone × hybrida (syn. *Anemone japonica*) 'Honorine Joubert'

This is the Japanese anemone that makes such a splendid contribution to the autumn garden. The more usual forms are rose pink, but there are variations in this colour and some fine whites including 'Honorine Joubert'. They can be invasive and are best planted as adjuncts to large shrubs that have flowered earlier in the year.

type	Herbaceous perennial
flowers	Large, flat, white
foliage	Broad, vine-like, dark green
height	1.5m (5ft)
spread	90cm (3ft)
hardiness	Hardy
planting	Plant in spring or late autumn
position	An open, sunny position
soil	Moisture retentive, limy or acid. Japanese anemones do not, on the whole, thrive on sandy, dry soils
propagation	By division in early spring, or root cuttings taken in midwinter and rooted in pots in a garden frame
alternatives	There are about twenty other varieties, of which the best are 'Queen Charlotte' and 'Louise Uhink' (pink) and 'White Giant' ('Géant des Blanches')

SCHIZOSTYLIS COCCINEA

SCHIZOSTYLIS
Schizostylis coccinea

This South African plant is often listed among bulbs but, although a member of the Iris family, its roots are a fibrous mat and not a bulb. It is not entirely hardy, as you might expect from its origins, but it is almost so, and will grow in all but the coldest areas as long as it is given the right conditions. It is pronounced 'skitso-steyelis' rather than the prevalent 'sheyezo-steyelis'.

type	Herbaceous perennial
flowers	Rich, bright crimson, resembling a lily or a gladiolus
foliage	Upright, slender, iris-like
height	60cm (2ft)
spread	30cm (1ft)
hardiness	Hardier than often thought, but not for the coldest areas. Spreads freely where it is really mild
planting	Plant in spring
position	Full sun, but needs a good deal of moisture
soil	Any good soil except sand or shallow soils over soft limestone
propagation	By division in spring. Each portion should carry four to six shoots
varieties	A choice of varieties, starting with the pink 'Tambara' in late summer,

and finishing with 'Viscountess Byng' in late autumn, provides a long flowering season and colours from soft rose to richest crimson

RUDBECKIA
Rudbeckia 'Goldsturm'

One of the boldest splashes of rich yellow that can be found to offset the red-purple palette of early autumn will be found among the perennial rudbeckias. They are related to *Echinacea* and share its elevated flower centre and slightly drooping petals.

type	Herbaceous perennial
flowers	Large, bold, deep yellow daisies with chocolate-brown to black centres
foliage	A little coarse, deep green
height	90cm (3ft)
spread	60cm (2ft)
hardiness	Hardy
planting	Plant in spring
position	Full sun
soil	Any good garden soil that is fairly moisture retentive
propagation	By division in spring
alternatives	'Goldquelle' is earlier, 'Golden Glow' is tall, coarse and brassy
special comment	A first-class foil for Michaelmas daisies

tasks

FOR THE

month

2

PROPAGATION

CUTTINGS FROM TENDER PLANTS

Almost all tender perennials and quite a few tender shrubs growing outdoors can be propagated this month from cuttings, with the specific aim of obtaining replacement plants should there be winter losses.

Some of the cuttings, such as those from osteospermums, will be quite soft. It may seem odd to be taking cuttings that are soft or only just semi-ripe at this time of year, but propagation possibilities are far more flexible than many people think, and as long as the material is in a condition in which it will root, little else matters.

As you are not looking for a large increase, the method used might as well be kept as simple as possible. For such plants as osteospermums, *Euryops pectinatus* and the more tender penstemons, a pot of 50/50 by volume of sand and peat on the kitchen windowsill will do perfectly well. After inserting the cuttings, take two hoops of wire, stand them in the compost, invert a plastic bag over them, draw it tight round the bottom of the pot, and you have a mini-propagator.

Cuttings of the more tender hebes, such as 'Alicia Amherst', 'La Séduisante' and *H. andersonii* 'Variegata', will root in boxes of pure sand in a cold frame and will be sturdy plants with quite large root systems by spring.

FUCHSIA STANDARDS

Fuchsia cuttings can be taken now for growing into standards. The cuttings will be semi-ripe but can be rooted either under mist or in a heated propagator. They will root quickly and should be potted on as soon as

---

possible and kept growing in heat.

As they grow, the leading shoot of each is encouraged to make swift progress by pinching out each sideshoot as it forms. The sideshoots are made in the angles of stem leaves, and these are left on. You should take care to remove just the sideshoots and not the leaves that subtend them, otherwise the plants will have no foliage with which to make food by the action of light.

DIVIDING PERENNIALS

Just as in spring, you can now propagate flowered herbaceous perennials by division, using much the same method as you did then. However, you should not break the plants down into divisions as small as those you can make earlier in the year, as they need substantial roots to see them through the winter and into spring growth.

DIVIDING ALPINES

The same goes for alpines. However, although I know it

to be so in theory, this book is based on personal experience, and I have to admit that in over a decade as an alpine nurseryman, during which time I propagated many hundreds of thousands of plants, I cannot recall ever having divided alpines in autumn. For whatever reason seemed right at the time, all the divisions were done in spring, so it would ill behove me to advise anything different. Mainly, I suppose, it was because to break down an alpine into commercially small pieces was not a good idea in autumn. There is probably no reason at all why larger divisions should not be made in autumn, apart from the general tendency of alpines to have root systems that are more wandering, longer, and less relatively compact than those of the larger plants of the border.

PLANNING

ROSES

This is your last chance to plan the planting of roses, as you should make out your orders and get them posted, otherwise you will be at the back of the queue.

You should decide what you want the roses for, rather than going through a catalogue and picking out the ones that catch your eye. Roses fulfil many roles in gardens, and your planning will dictate which parts your roses will be called upon to play. It is a good idea to have an overall idea of the types of roses and their uses.

Bush roses

These are the hybrid teas and floribundas. They are best grown in beds of their own, as they are different from other kinds of plants. Because of the way they are pruned, they behave in much the same way as summer-flowering herbaceous plants, but fail to mix happily with them. With bush roses, colour is paramount, and no matter what care you give to the selection of flower size and quality, you will always find yourself working out colour schemes and finding roses to fit them. This is perfectly valid, but bush roses are isolationist in their demands.

Modern shrub roses

Shrub roses in general fit much more readily into mixed plantings, chiefly because they are shrubs like any others and not annually renewed, stiff frameworks entirely for the display of flowers. They have characteristics of shape, habit and foliage that give them value even when not in flower.

A shrub rose of a given colour can perform as the centrepiece for a group of different kinds of plants based on that colour, and you may need only half a dozen or so to lend coherence to quite a large border.

Old-fashioned roses

These are shrub roses raised before the modern, perpetual-flowering hybrid teas and floribundas had been developed. They have all the advantages of modern shrub roses but many flower only once, in midsummer, and others repeat fairly poorly. They have wonderful fragrances, delightfully shaped, 'cabbagey' blooms, and pretty foliage, and many are not nearly as subject to disease as modern roses.

The old rose colours are quite different. They are on the whole more modest, less flamboyant, given to velvety maroons and even dove grey, and they should be regarded as shrubs in their own right. It is entirely illogical, for example, to grow a deutzia that flowers in early summer only and has no scent, and at the same time to give no room to an old-fashioned rose that will bloom for two months in summer and give a fragrant elegance to the garden that nothing else can in quite the same way.

English roses

These are a new race of roses, combining the virtues of the old-fashioned shrub roses with those of the modern bush roses. You can use them either on their own in a bed or as focal points in mixed plantings, or just grow them with other plants.

Species, climbing and rambling roses

These have their own particular uses, and your planning will include them according to whether you want to grow roses over walls, fences, trees, or – if you have a very large garden – just as flowering shrubs for the wilder areas.

plants
OF THE
month
2

SEDUM
Sedum 'Autumn Joy'

The large-headed sedums, forms or hybrids of *S. spectabile*, are indispensable assets to the autumn garden, both early and late. They are superb butterfly plants with the exception of 'Autumn Joy' which, though the most cleanly coloured, avoiding the puce of others, is a sterile hybrid and does not attract butterflies.

type	Herbaceous perennial
flowers	Large heads of tiny, starry flowers; rich pink, turning darker with age and eventually coppery red
foliage	Broad, grey-green, toothed, succulent
height	60cm (2ft)
spread	60cm (2ft)
hardiness	Hardy
planting	Plant in spring or late autumn
position	Full sun
soil	Any good garden soil
propagation	By division in spring
alternatives	*S. spectabile* 'Brilliant', *S.s.* 'Meteor'. 'Iceberg' is white

MICHAELMAS DAISY
Aster amellus 'Sternkugel'

The varieties of *Aster amellus* are sometimes included under the term Michaelmas daisy, but their flowering period starts in late summer and they are at their peak earlier than the true Michaelmas daisies (see below), which are at their best late in the month and well into next. *Aster amellus* are shorter, tough, fairly disease-resistant plants. They are also attractive to butterflies.

type	Woody-stemmed herbaceous perennial
flowers	Many-rayed daisies, rich lavender-pink
foliage	Matt, dull green
height	50cm (20in)
spread	30cm (1ft)
hardiness	Hardy
planting	Plant in spring or late autumn
position	Sun or part shade
soil	Any good garden soil
propagation	By division in spring
alternatives	About a dozen varieties, including 'Brilliant' (deep rose pink), 'Moerheim Gem' (violet), 'Sonia', pale pink

MICHAELMAS DAISY
Aster novi-belgii varieties

These, the New York asters, and the *novae-angliae* (New England) asters are the true Michaelmas daisies. Wisely chosen, their display can last from the middle of this month until late autumn.

type	Woody-stemmed herbaceous perennials
flowers	Many-rayed daisies in a variety of colours in the pink to purple range, including some good blues
foliage	Matt, dull green
height	75cm–1.5m (2½–5ft) according to variety
spread	45–65cm (18–26in)
hardiness	Hardy
planting	Plant in spring or late autumn
position	Full sun or part shade
soil	Any good garden soil, including moist
propagation	By division in spring
alternatives	There are many. It is advisable to buy from a specialist nursery and to ask for varieties known to be resistant to disease

SEDUM 'AUTUMN JOY'

ASTER NOVI-BELGII VARIETIES

PENSTEMON
Penstemon 'Raven'

Herbaceous, as opposed to shrubby, pen-stemons are late-flowering plants of the greatest value. Generally speaking, those with somewhat smaller, more slender flowers are the hardiest, while the wider, larger, tubbier ones tend to be less so. Some with very large flowers are, frankly, tender. The hardier ones (of which the bright red 'Garnet' is a fine example) often remain green all winter in mild areas and should not be cut down until spring; otherwise they are herbaceous, dying down later in the autumn but flowering well into next month.

type	Semi-herbaceous perennial (evergreen in mild areas)
flowers	Deep crimson, wide-tubular
foliage	Slender, bright green
height	75cm (30in)
spread	60cm (2ft)
hardiness	Will stand a considerable amount of severe winter cold but not cold, dry spring winds
planting	Plant in spring or late autumn
position	Full sun, shelter from cold winds
soil	Any good garden soil
propagation	By softwood cuttings in late spring
alternatives	'Garnet' is deep red; 'King George' is crimson with a white throat; 'Myddleton Gem' is light red; 'Firebird' is scarlet; 'Sour Grapes' is greenish purple (plants labelled 'Sour Grapes' are often, in fact, 'Stapleford Gem')

plants
IN
flower

KEY

= evergreen   spp = species
vars = varieties

NOTES

Ceratostigma griffithii and *Grevillea* 'Sulphurea'
are tender. *Oxydendrum arboreum* requires
lime-free soil.

TREES	colour	flower type
*Magnolia grandiflora	Creamy white	Very large, fragrant
Oxydendrum arboreum	White	Urn shaped, in drooping clusters

SHRUBS		
Abelia × grandiflora	White, pink tinge	Small, funnel shaped
Aralia elata	White	Small, in large plumes
Ceratostigma griffithii	Deep blue	Plumbago-like
Elsholzia stauntonii	Deep lilac	Pea shaped, in large bunches
*Eucryphia 'Nymansay'	White	Saucer shaped
*Grevillea 'Sulphurea'	Yellow	Tubular, like honeysuckle
Lespedeza thunbergii	Rose-purple	Pea shaped
Perovskia atriplicifolia	Lavender-blue	Tubular, lipped

Also: ***Buddleia, Calluna, Ceratostigma willmottianum, Clerodendrum, Colutea, Daboecia cantabrica, Erica*** spp, ***Fuchsia, Hebe, Hibiscus, Hydrangea, Hypericum, Genista tinctoria, Indigofera, Leycesteria formosa, Potentilla, Romneya, Yucca.***

CLIMBERS		
Polygonum baldschuanicum (Russian vine)	White	Large plumes
Solanum crispum 'Glasnevin'	Purple or white	Like potato flowers

Also: ***Campsis, Clematis, Eccremocarpus, Jasminum, Lapageria, Mutisia, Passiflora, Pileostegia***

EASY ON THE EYE

During early autumn, the borders behave rather like a crowd at the end of a football match. One moment they are at their fullest, bursting with colour and activity; the next sees them having almost imperceptibly thinned, and after a short while you realise that a steady drift home has become established.

Your eye once more becomes attuned, as it was in spring and early summer before the great rush of flowering that was to come later, to individual colour matches and contrasts, and to the importance of flower shape and size. The white, fluffy-centred *Leucanthemum superbum* 'Snowcap', a short-stemmed form of what used until recently to be *Chrysanthemum maximum*, growing intimately with the crimson, double, equally fluffy nasturtium *Tropaeolum majus* 'Hermione Grashoff', is just the sort of association that easily passes unnoticed in high summer but begins to catch the eye as other distractions disappear.

MAGNOLIAS IN AUTUMN

Magnolia grandiflora is a tree magnolia. In its native south-eastern United States it grows very large, often to more than 30m (100ft), especially on the drier 'Hammocks' of the swamps. Like yuccas, it is hardy but cannot stand up to the weight of snow, and for that reason it never grows to large sizes in cool-temperate climates, where its branches break and flowering is attenuated. While still young, it is not so susceptible to breakage and will flower well, but only if you choose a variety that flowers at an early age. 'Exmouth' and 'Goliath' are the ones to look for; note the brown-felted undersides of the leaves in the former, but not the latter, whose leaves are green on both sides. The best long-term results with this magnolia species are with trees that have been trained from youth on sheltered walls that are not too hot. It will grow happily and for very many years on a good, rich soil and, provided that there is plenty of organic matter added, will thrive over chalk.

For sheer size of flower and delicacy of scent, *Magnolia grandiflora* has no rival in the garden in late summer and early autumn, and I would rather plant it than any of the somewhat hackneyed magnolias of spring, were I to be allowed only the one.

PERENNIALS	colour	height
Ceratostigma plumbaginoides	Dark blue	30cm (12in)
Cimicifuga cordifolia	White	1.2m (48in)
Aster amellus vars	Various	60cm (24in)
Aster × *frikartii* 'Mönch'	Blue	90cm (36in)
novae-angliae vars	Various	60cm–1.5m (24–60in)
novi-belgii vars	Various	90cm–1.5m (36in–60in)
Penstemon many	Various	75cm (30in)
Schizostylis coccinea vars	Pink, white or red	60cm (24in)
Sedum maximum 'Atropurpureum'	Deep pink	45cm (18in)
'Vera Jameson'	Pale pink	25cm (10in)
Campanula portenschlagiana	Blue	15cm (6in)

Also: **Anaphalis, Anemone × hybrida, Centaurea, Centranthus, Coreopsis, Crocosmia, Dianthus, Eryngium, Geranium, Gypsophila, Helenium, Heliopsis, Hemerocallis, Heuchera, Hosta, Kniphofia, Lavatera, Liatris, Ligularia, Limonium, Lythrum, Monarda, Oenothera, Phlox, Physostegia, Polygonum, Potentilla, Rudbeckia, Salvia, Scabiosa, Silene schafta, Stokesia, Tradescantia, Veronica, Zauschneria.**

BULBS

	colour	height
Colchicum spp	Lilac, mauve or pink	10–18cm (4–7½in)
Crocus cancellatus	Lilac, marked purple	12cm (5in)
cartwrightianus	Purple	8cm (3in)
Scilla autumnalis	Lilac	10cm (4in)
Sternbergia lutea	Yellow	12cm (5in)

ROCK GARDEN

Ceratostigma plumbaginoides
Colchicum spp
Crocus see bulbs
Gentiana – Asiatic spp and hybs
Lapeirousia cruenta
Sternbergia lutea
Zauschneria microphylla

THE NEGLECTED SEASON

The plant associations of spring have much in common with those of early autumn and those of neither season receive the attention lavished upon those of summer. Much is written about colour co-ordination, themes and harmonies, but almost always with the summer border in mind. When summer is over, there remain nine months before the next one. What a short-sighted view it is that takes no heed of the importance of plant associations during that long period!

THE TIDY TIME

No matter what else is said about plant associations for September, remember that it is the *only* time in the whole year when bare, freshly cultivated soil among the plants looks positively attractive (because of the contrast with the busyness of August). Clean out everything tatty, dying or dead and do not be in too much of a hurry to fill in the spaces. Give yourself some thinking time.

PLAN FOR BULBS

There are many such autumnal combinations that should be deliberately planned for a full year ahead. It is such long-range plans, when there is a considerable time lag between conception, ordering the plants, planting them and then their flowering, that are impossible to execute coherently unless you make use of a methodically kept notebook.

You will now be planting the spring bulbs. Yet on what grounds have you planned their deployment? Have you just seen nice ones in pictures at the garden centre or in the catalogue and thought in general, perhaps woolly terms that they would look good? Or did you, last spring when bulb time was at its height, go out and look at other gardens, public and private, notebook in hand?

For you cannot even set bulbs, stand back, assess the effect, and then rearrange them. You make holes, put them in, and cannot see them any more. They are gone until next spring. This is why you so often see dreary lines of otherwise lovely daffodils slavishly following the edge of a drive, and it is why scillas and crocuses, appearing in isolated clumps on rockeries, make you feel even colder by their naked vulnerability to the chilly winds, unsheltered by the friendly warmth of neighbouring plants.

OCTOBER

There is no season when such pleasant and sunny
spots may be lighted on, and produce so pleasant
an effect on the feelings, as now in October.

NATHANIEL HAWTHORNE

*This month is true autumn, temperamental and hardly to be
trusted, but capable of the utmost charm as well as the most
dreadful rages. There are wild gales and lashing rain, but there
are also still, diamond days after crisp frosts, when views you
had forgotten about appear again with the fall of leaves,
sharpened by the sun's clarity in the rain-washed air.*

*Just as in spring there is a rush to flower before the deciduous
canopy closes overhead, now there is another, lesser scramble, as
it falls away. There is little to compare with the sight of freshly
opened autumn crocuses, leafless on the lawn's edge, standing like
footless wine glasses magically balanced by some mischievous,
overnight hand.*

*Colchicums flop foolishly after a few days, but are always
endearing.* Cyclamen hederifolium *can be found all over the
world where it can enjoy a cool, leafy spot. It is valued almost as
much for its marbled leaves as for its sturdy blooms that never
bow, even before the strongest winds.*

*This month is prized by many for the colours of the autumn
leaves, but in equable climates they can often be mediocre. They
can also be fleeting, swept away by gales before they can be
appreciated. It is therefore a mistake to give the autumn garden
over to a celebration of foliage colours.*

Nevertheless, to dismiss them completely is as great an error.

*Autumn's glory is a fuchsia's clear scarlet against the burnt-
orange leaves of a dogwood. It is deep, velvety-crimson nicotianas
beside a flaming Japanese Maple, inwardly lit nerines against the
last deep green of a shrub rose, and the rosy-lilac saffron crocus,
orange-red stigmas echoing its bed of fallen leaves.*

tasks

FOR THE

month

1

PLANT SUPPORTS
Once herbaceous plants have
finished flowering, remove, dry,
clean and store their supports. If
you used twiggy sticks, burn
them before they can harbour
fungus diseases.

CHECKLIST

- ☐ Continue to cut back herbaceous perennials Remove all weeds from among their crowns
- ☐ Rake or pick up all fallen leaves from lawns and beds and compost them. Do *not* burn
- ☐ Later in the month, lift and store dahlias if necessary
- ☐ Protect young evergreen shrubs from wind
- ☐ Finish pruning rambler roses
- ☐ Plant spring bedding, containerised trees and shrubs, and bulbs, especially tulips
- ☐ Plant up your new rock garden

MAINTENANCE

WEEDING PERENNIALS

You are quite likely to find that pernicious weeds have seeded into your border and gained a hold among the crowns of the herbaceous perennials. You will not have noticed them because of the top growth, but now they become obvious. It is very tempting, when you have removed the greater part of such a weed, to give up and leave a little behind. This will cause you untold trouble, as the next time you notice it will be a full year later, by which time it may have killed out the plant, if not its immediate neighbours.

In such cases, lift the border plant and tease every last piece of weed root away from the roots of the plant. You will be surprised just how much there will probably be and how deep it has managed to run.

BONFIRES VERSUS COMPOST

There has been much to-do about bonfires recently. Garden bonfires are unlikely to make the slightest

difference to global warming, and you should have no compunction about burning material that might cause disease, weed roots, dead wood, and so on. Thinking 'green' people will rightly maintain, however, that to burn material which can be made into good compost or mulch is – given the state of our increased knowledge of ecological balances, plain common sense and elementary home economics – verging on the criminal.

DAHLIAS

If your climate is on the cold side, leave dahlias blackened by the first air frost for a few days until their tops have died right down.

- ■ Cut the stems to within 15cm (6in) of the ground.

- ■ Insert the spade into the soil about 30cm (1ft) from the centre of a plant and, with one hand on the spade and the other on the stem stumps, gently ease the tuber from the ground.

- ■ Discard any broken tubers and bring the sound ones under frost-free cover, where they should be turned upside down so as to drain the hollow stems.

WARNING

■ *If you cut the stems too short, you risk damaging the points where new growth is made; too long and they are unlikely to drain properly and will get in the way* ■

- ■ Once drained, place the tubers right way up in boxes of moss peat that is just damp, leaving the crowns uncovered.

- ■ Inspect the tubers at intervals between now and spring, cutting any diseased parts back to sound tissues and dusting with sulphur.

- ■ Some tubers will shrivel. Put them in a bucket of water overnight and then dry them thoroughly before returning them to store.

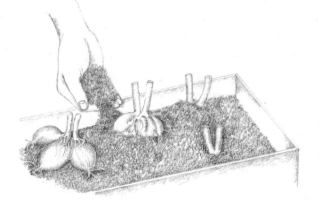

EVERGREEN SHRUBS

Take this point further and erect netting protection for young evergreen shrubs. The object is not to exclude the wind, but merely to slow it and reduce its wind-chill factor. If you also mulch them on a warmish day, you will retain soil warmth as well as moisture, and the plants will have just a little longer to make root growth.

PLANTING

BULBS

You should finish your bulb planting this month. Tulips can be left until quite late in the month, but everything else should be in as soon as possible.

EVERGREENS

Evergreen shrubs are not, on the whole, easy to establish. Many losses, attributed to tenderness, are really caused by an insufficient understanding of their needs.

The survival of a plant is dictated by the fact that the water lost by its leaves must never exceed the water gained by its roots. This means that if you plant in autumn, you stand the risk of its dying because cold, drying winds draw the moisture from the leaves while the roots, made partly dormant by the soil temperature, cannot supply enough to compensate.

In spring, the danger to newly planted evergreens is twofold. There may be cold, continental winds that can be fiercely drying, and also there will be an increasing amount of warmth and sunshine to counteract the

action of the roots.

The main solution to the problems of both seasons is to mulch as soon after planting as possible, using at least a 5cm (2in) depth of partly rotted organic matter or something like composted forest bark. The secondary remedy is to temper the wind to the young plant (see above), and the third is to water when it becomes necessary. Watering has little or no effect from now until mid-spring.

There is nothing like the same problem with deciduous trees and shrubs, some of which may in fact be less temperature-hardy than evergreens but do not have to cope with the loss of water to anything like the same degree. The drying caused by cold winds is termed 'physiological drought' and is a major killer in the garden.

SPRING BEDDING

Plant out bedding for next spring. The plants used for bedding are mainly biennials, they have made their growth

but no flowers this year, and will flower and die next year.

ROCK GARDEN

If you made a rock garden earlier and have been waiting for the soil to settle, you can plant it during the first half of the month, but you must be prepared from the outset always to inspect the plants after any severe frost. This is because the action of the frost will be to lift the plants partly from the soil, and the better and more gritty your soil, the more likely it is to happen.

A good top-dressing of pebbles is an excellent precaution against frost and has saved many an autumn-planted alpine. Do not forget that the majority of alpines are evergreen and used to being comfortably ensconced beneath snow. They are not accustomed by nature to drying, frosty winds in winter. The best precaution, again, is the mulch, as it prevents the freezing of the roots that prevents their taking up water to replace that lost by the leaves.

SOIL TEMPERATURE
Plant growth stops when the temperature of the soil drops below 5°C (41°F). This is also the temperature at which the anomalous expansion of water begins, culminating in the formation of ice.

SPRING BEDDING PLANTS

Bellis (Double daisies)
Campanula medium
(Canterbury bells)
Cheiranthus (wallflowers)
Dianthus barbatus
(Sweet Williams)
Myosotis (forget-me-nots)
Polyanthus
Winter-flowering pansies

plants
OF THE
month
1

CHRYSANTHEMUM
Argyranthemum 'Jamaica Primrose'

While not a true autumn flower – it blooms for most of the summer – 'Jamaica Primrose' is outstanding now before the harder frosts kill it. It is especially fine when allowed to thread its stems among grey foliage. Until recently it was classified as a chrysanthemum.

type	Tender perennial
flowers	Large, yellow daisies
foliage	Green, ferny
height	45cm (18in)
spread	45cm (18in)
hardiness	Not winter-hardy, but will withstand light frosts
planting	Plant in spring after danger of frosts has passed
position	Full sun
soil	Not too rich, well drained
propagation	Take shoots a few inches long early in the month and root them in 50/50 sand and moss peat by volume. Pot up when rooted and overwinter in a frost-free greenhouse
alternatives	*Argyranthemum frutescens* (marguerite) has white flowers

ARGYRANTHEMUM 'JAMAICA PRIMROSE'

CYCLAMEN
Cyclamen hederifolium

By choosing well from the species of cyclamen, it is possible to have flowers for many months of the year. *C. hederifolium* (syn. *C. neapolitanum*) is valuable for its comparatively long flowering season and for its beautifully marbled leaves, which follow the first flowers and coincide with the later ones. Flowering may begin as early as midsummer, there are often blooms a month later, early autumn sees the species into full flower, and this month the combined beauty of flowers and foliage is at its peak. This sequence varies with latitude and climate, and may be compressed into early to mid-autumn.

type	Tuberous perennial
flowers	Auricled (notched), recurved, rose pink to white
foliage	Oval, ivy or arrow shaped, smooth edged or wavy, matt green marbled with silver to varying degrees. The leaves of no two individuals are alike
height	10–12cm (4–5in)
spread	Old tubers may bear up to fifty flowers and be 15cm (6in) or even more across

hardiness	Hardy
planting	Plant when dormant in mid- to late summer or at any time when purchased pot-grown 'in the green'
position	Partly shaded
soil	A good garden soil with well-rotted organic matter added
propagation	By seed preferably sown as soon as it is ripe. All species germinate at the same time of year as the leaves appear on adult plants
special comment	Mulching during the dormant period is important for this species, as it is surface-rooting from the top of the tuber

COLCHICUM
Colchicum autumnale

Although colchicums are all too frequently called 'autumn crocuses', they are nothing of the sort, and the crocus species of autumn are entirely different. Crocuses have corms, colchicums have tubers; crocuses have three stamens, colchicums have six. They flower incredibly quickly from tubers in early autumn and then appear reliably every year thereafter, increasing freely as time passes.

type	'Bulb' – in fact tuberous
flowers	Long-necked, large goblets, rosy-mauve
foliage	Large, strap-shaped, produced after flowering
height	15cm (6in)
spread	Clumps increase rapidly
hardiness	Hardy
planting	Plant when available in late summer or early autumn
position	Flowers best in full sun, but looks best beside shrubs or near small trees
soil	Any reasonable garden soil
propagation	By division of the clumps in late summer
special comment	The flowers of many colchicum species fall over a few days after opening. This happens in the best weather and is not a sign of pests or disease

NERINE
Nerine bowdenii

The gorgeous nerines of autumn are like no other flowers. The petals contain cells that behave like crystals, reflecting and concentrating

NERINE BOWDENII

the light so that they seem to glow from within as if made from cool jewellery. They take a year or two to settle down, but should then be left to increase undisturbed for many years, as they flower best when crowded.

type	Bulbous perennial
flowers	Ice-pink, petals strap-shaped and undulating
foliage	Strap shaped
height	60cm (2ft)
spread	30cm (1ft)
hardiness	Hardy in most areas if sheltered from cold winds
planting	Plant in late summer, 15cm (6in) deep
position	The foot of a warm wall is the classic position for nerines, but it should not be hot and dry. In my own experience, the base of a shrub rose, where they received a little shade during the day, proved eminently successful, as did a formal bed in a tiny town garden
propagation	By division of established clumps, or removal of bulbils, in late summer. These should be transplanted to pots or a nursery bed
alternatives	Other species are best treated as greenhouse plants

tasks

FOR THE

month

2

SHRUBS TO PROPAGATE

Among the genera that can be propagated from hardwood cuttings in the open are:

Azara • Buddleia
Campsis • Celtis
Deutzia • Diervilla
Escallonia (in mild areas)
Forsythia • Franklinia
Jasminum • Kerria
Laburnum • Leycesteria
Ligustrum • Metasequoia
Neillia • Philadelphus
Physocarpus
Platanus • Populus
Prunus cerasifera vars
Rhodotypos
Ribes • Salix
Sambucus • Santolina
Sorbaria • Spiraea
Stephanandra
Symphoricarpos
Tamarix
Viburnum (deciduous)
Vitis
Weigela

CHECKLIST ✓

☐ Divide herbaceous perennials
☐ Take hardwood cuttings of shrubs and roses
☐ Take leaf-bud cuttings of mahonias
☐ Plan the planting of spring-flowering perennials

PROPAGATION

RENOVATING OLD BORDER PLANTS

At some time or other you are almost certain to find yourself with some real old stagers among the herbaceous plants. They form seemingly impenetrable masses of root that have about as much sympathy to handling as barbed wire, and you feel you should really divide them, but shirk the job — yet again.

■ If you have such a plant, dig it up and lay the root ball on ground — not on a path or on concrete, but soil that has not recently been dug.

■ As you are a good gardener, your spade will be clean and shiny, but it is worth honing it to a reasonable cutting edge with the sort of stone that is used for grass hooks and scythes.

■ Using all your weight through hands and foot, thrust the spade through the middle of the root ball, slicing down into the soil beneath.

■ Separate the two halves and cut them in their turn into halves.

■ Do nothing more at this stage other than to plant the four quarters as they are.

■ Not next spring but the one following, by which time the quarters will have put on strong, new crowns and roots, dig them up again and divide them. This time, discard the older parts and just replant the young growths.

By following this process, instead of one old, failing plant, you will have about a dozen young, strong ones eager to make a fine floral display.

SHRUBS FROM HARDWOOD CUTTINGS

Many deciduous shrubs, particularly, as it happens, the most popular ones, can be propagated by the simplest method of all, which is to take cuttings of fully ripe wood this month.

It is quite astonishing that amateur gardeners almost totally ignore this method, which calls for no special equipment whatever, not even a frame in most cases. Take a spade, some coarse sand, your secateurs and a spare bit of ground, and you are in business.

■ A hardwood cutting is made from a fully ripened shoot of the current year's wood. The bark should be completely hard and will not wrinkle and pull away under pressure from your thumb. How long the cutting is will depend on the distance between the buds, but most are around 25cm (10in) or a little less. You can, of course, use prunings.

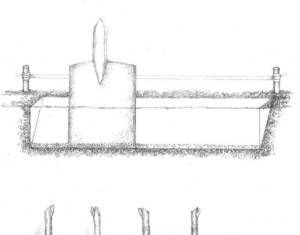

25cms.

■ Cut straight across below a joint (bud), and then make a sloping cut just above a bud higher up. You will usually find the ends of the shoots too soft, and will discard the terminal bud. By always making the low cut straight and the high cut sloping, you will avoid the embarrassment of putting your cuttings in upside down.

■ Dip the bases of the cuttings in hormone rooting powder and tap off the excess.

■ Make a trench in your spare piece of ground, which should be in shelter, by driving the spade in vertically and rocking it forward. Use the sharp sand to make a layer about 2.5cm (1in) deep at the bottom.

■ Rest the bases of the cuttings on the sand at 15cm (6in) intervals and backfill the trench, firming with your foot. The lower two-thirds of each cutting should be in the soil.

■ Loosen the soil surface where you trod, otherwise puddling will occur.

■ Keep weeds down during the following spring and summer and leave the cuttings until autumn, when they can be dug up and planted in permanent quarters.

■ The cuttings are inserted, one to a pot, so that the stem section is just buried in the 50/50 peat/sand compost. Rooting is slow and should take place in a heated propagating frame or, best of all, in a mist unit.

■ You will know that the cuttings are rooted when, next spring, you see a robust new shoot pushing up through the soil of each pot.

■ When it is growing well, you can trim away the old leaf, as its work is done.

ROSES FROM HARDWOOD CUTTINGS

Most roses other than bush roses (hybrid teas and floribundas) and climbers can quite easily be propagated from hardwood cuttings. I have used the method to greatest effect with old-fashioned shrub roses and ramblers.

■ The cuttings should be taken as late as possible, towards the end of this month or even during next.

■ Hardwood cuttings of roses are not usually very long and will root if they are as short as 10cm (4in), although 15cm (6in) is better if shoots of that length can be found.

■ The tips are usually on the soft side and should be clipped off to a bud and discarded, but the cuttings may well have a few leaves even so late in the year. It is best to leave them alone and let them fall in their own time.

■ It is sometimes recommended that you remove the prickles, but it is not necessary and is only for your own comfort. Wear gloves and you should have no trouble.

■ The cuttings should be given the same length of time in which to root as other hardwood cuttings.

■ Hybrid teas and floribundas will root from hardwood cuttings, but the resulting plants tend to be weaker than those grafted onto commercial rootstocks. It can, however, be worth doing with a select few of the more vigorous varieties and with many modern shrub roses.

MAHONIAS FROM CUTTINGS

You can propagate mahonias this month. Many people shy away from doing so because they cannot see how to take cuttings from them. In fact, you take leaf-bud cuttings.

■ Each cutting consists of an entire, pinnate leaf, a section of the stem to which it is attached, and the bud in the axil between the leaf and stem. The leaf can be reduced in size by about one-third to prevent toppling.

NOTE

■ *Some gardeners (I am among them) cut the stem section longitudinally in half, discarding the part without the leaf. I have to admit that I am not entirely clear why I do this, only that I always have, which is no good reason at all, but it gets good results* ■

■ The stems should be green and semi-ripe, as they are this month, and not brown and ripe, as are those of many other shrubs. The length of stem attached to the cutting should be about 5cm (2in).

PLANNING

PLAN FOR SPRING

The most valuable planning you can do this month is to bear spring in mind while you are tidying the borders. Almost all gardeners overemphasise summer in their flower borders, and spring among their shrubs. At the risk of labouring the point, one must say that good gardening is a matter of balance, and you should turn a critical eye on the borders and see if you should not plan to include more spring-flowering perennials.

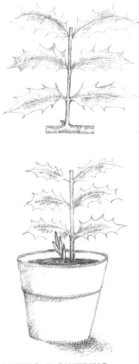

MAHONIA CUTTINGS

SPRING-FLOWERING PERENNIALS

Bergenia
Doronicum
Epimedium
Euphorbia
Helleborus
Pulmonaria

plants
OF THE
month
2

▼
DAHLIA
Dahlia 'Bishop of Llandaff'

This is the month during which dahlias seem to put extra energy into flowering, as if they somehow know that their long days of blooming are almost over. Ground frosts do not affect them much, but the first air frost will see them blackened and ready for lifting for the winter in the colder areas. In mild climates dahlias will overwinter in the garden. During these last weeks, dahlias are rendered the more conspicuous by the dying down of their hardier neighbours.

type	Peony-flowered border dahlia
flowers	Brilliant scarlet, late summer onwards
foliage	Deep bronze-maroon
height	Varies according to conditions, 90cm–1.5m (3–5ft)
spread	Also varies. Plants in full leaf cover up to 1sq m (1sq yd)
hardiness	In climates where the soil does not become frozen solid below about 2cm (¾in), and that only fairly occasionally, this and similar dahlias may safely be left in the ground all year. In colder climates they should be lifted after the first blackening frost and prepared for storage in a frost-free building
planting	Plant the tubers 10cm (4in) deep in spring when the dangers of hard frosts are past. Tie the stems loosely to stakes 30cm (1ft) shorter than their final heights
position	Full sun
soil	Any good, well-drained soil, enriched well in advance with well-rotted manure. Give a light dressing (100gm per sq m/3oz per sq yd) of bonemeal when planting
propagation	By division of the tubers in early spring. Place them in a shallow box containing a moist mixture of equal parts of moss peat and sand. After fourteen to twenty days, the eyes will swell. Divide the tubers by cutting with a sharp knife so that each division has at least one eye. Dust the cut surfaces with sulphur and plant out the divisions
alternatives	A recent introduction, 'Bednall Beauty' is shorter and more compact

▶
CHINESE LANTERN
Physalis franchetii
(syn. *P. alkengi* var. *franchetii*)

Many flower arrangers love to grow this plant for its unique, bright orange seed pods that can be such a feature of the flower garden in autumn. They are delightful in a simple arrangement with honesty or complementing the berries of *Iris foetidissima*, or as part of a general autumn arrangement. Needless to say, they make a bright focal point in the garden.

type	Herbaceous perennial
flowers	Insignificant, cream. It is the orange-red seed pods ('Chinese lanterns') for which the plant is grown
foliage	Lanceolate, mid-green
height	60cm (2ft)
spread	90cm (3ft)
hardiness	Hardy
planting	Spring or late autumn

DAHLIA 'BISHOP OF LLANDAFF'

PHYSALIS FRANCHETII

position	Full sun
soil	Any good border soil
propagation	By division in spring or root cuttings in winter

SAXIFRAGE
Saxifraga fortunei

This plant is remarkably different from most garden saxifrages, but is still most at home among rocks and in a gritty soil. It is too tall and its leaves too large for a small rock garden, but a partly shaded place on a larger one is ideal.

type	Deciduous (herbaceous) alpine (perennial)
flowers	White. Each has five petals; the two lower ones are three to four times as long as the upper three
foliage	Bold, rounded, glossy, brownish green, the undersides and leaf stalks conspicuously red
height	40cm (16in) in flower
spread	30cm (12in)
hardiness	Hardy
planting	Whenever available
position	Part shade, cool
soil	Leafy, gritty
propagation	By division in spring
varieties	'Wada', large, purple leaves; 'Rubrifolia', leaves reddish brown

MONKSHOOD
Aconitum carmichaelii

There are several species of monkshoods, all of which bear a 'family' resemblance, with hooded flowers in some shade of blue or near-blue and divided leaves. The roots are poisonous, hence the folk name 'Wolfsbane'. This species is the latest in flower and maintains its foliage well, although a certain amount of yellowing is inevitable in a plant that comes into leaf very early in the year.

type	Herbaceous perennial
flowers	Upright, hooded, in spikes. Blue to violet-blue
foliage	Wide, divided leaves
height	1.2cm (4ft)
spread	30cm (1ft)
hardiness	Hardy
planting	Plant in late autumn or winter
position	Full sun, part or full shade
soil	Any good soil, preferably moisture retentive but well drained
propagation	By division in late autumn. 'Barker's Variety' comes true from seed
varieties	'Arendsii', rich blue; 'Barker's Variety', good blue, tall; 'Kelmscott', deep violet blue; *A.c. wilsonii*, over 1.5m (5ft)

plants

IN

flower

KEY

* = evergreen   spp = species

vars = varieties

TREES	colour	flower type
*Magnolia grandiflora	Creamy white	Very large, fragrant

SHRUBS	colour	flower type
*Erica carnea early vars	Various	Heather
*Fatsia japonica	White	Round clusters
Mahonia × media vars	Yellow	Long racemes

Also: **Abelia, Calluna, Ceratostigma, Erica vagans, Fuchsia, Hibiscus, Hydrangea, Hypericum, Lespedeza, Potentilla**

CLIMBERS

Clematis, Eccremocarpus scaber, Lapageria rosea

PERENNIALS

Anemone × hybrida, Aster amellus, Aster novae-angliae, Aster novi-belgii, Ceratostigma plumbaginoides, Heliopsis, Kniphofia, Liriope muscari, Polygonum, Rudbeckia, Scabiosa, Schizostylis, Silene schafta

BULBS	colour	height	remarks
Colchicum agrippinum	Violet, chequered	10cm (4in)	
atropurpureum	White, becoming carmine-purple	7cm (2½in)	
'Autumn Queen'	Lilac	15cm (6in)	
autumnale			
album plenum	Double, white	15cm (6in)	Rare
pleniflorum	Double, mauve	10cm (4in)	
cilicum	Rosy-lilac	7cm (2½in)	

PLANTS FOR ORNAMENTAL FRUIT

This month is the peak of the season of 'mellow fruitfulness' and the well-planned garden will always have a good display of various fruits. In this context 'fruit' is not restricted to those that are edible, but includes any seed-bearing organs that are of ornamental value. There is a dramatic decline in flowering as compared with the previous month, and the colour factor is to a large extent taken over by fruits. This is also true of next month, which is, in climates where winters are not dominated by snow, the nadir of the flowering year.

Continentally-influenced climates will, from now onwards, to a greater or lesser extent remain flowerless until the general spring thaw, but milder, maritime or island climates will see a thread of flowering activity continuing until the year 'starts' again in early spring. In these latter locations, which include the British Isles, this month may be seen as the end of the main flowering phase of the year, next month as a transitional, almost blank time, and the following month as the start of low-key, winter flowering that is none the less often quite ravishing.

Trees

Crataegus Although the hawthorns are among the best-known berrying trees, they are all too often planted without proper concern for the lasting and attractive qualities of their berries. Among the best for berries are *Crataegus laciniata*, which has large, coral-red fruits, and *C. × lavallei* 'Carrieri', whose leaves are among the last to fall of all trees, and whose orange-red berries last right through winter. Several forms of the common hawthorn, *C. monogyna*, bear heavy crops of red fruits, often referred to as 'haws', as opposed to 'hips', which are the fruits of roses.

Ilex There are too many berried hollies to list. Practically all female hollies have berries, usually red, but sometimes yellow, and there are also black-berried hollies. It is best to buy hollies for their foliage and to consider the berries as secondary, as quantities vary from year to year but their evergreen foliage is always decorative. Beware of thinking that 'Golden Queen' is female, as it is male; 'Golden King', on the other hand, is not male . . . but female.

Magnolia Several magnolias bear fruit. Typically, they look like long, thick, extremely warty sausages, which split open to reveal a

ROCK GARDEN

Crocus spp
Cyclamen cilicium
Cyclamen hederifolium
Erica carnea – **early vars**
Galanthus reginae-olgae
Gentiana – **Asiatic spp and hybs**
Zauschneria microphylla

	colour	height
'Rosy Dawn'	Pink	15cm (6in)
speciosum	Purple, white centre	15cm (6in)
album	White	15cm (6in)

The following **colchicums** flower a month earlier:
autumnale, lilac, 15cm (6in); ***bornmülleri***, violet, 18cm (7½in); ***byzantinum***, rosy-lilac, 15cm (6in); **'The Giant'**, large, lilac-mauve, 25cm (10in); **'Violet Queen'**, purple, 15cm (6in); **'Water Lily'**, large, double, rosy-lilac, 10cm (4in).

Crocus hadriaticus	Large, creamy white	10cm (4in)
karduchorum	Pale lavender-pink	12cm (5in)
medius	Lilac-purple	8cm (3in)
nudiflorus	Deep violet	15cm (6in)
pulchellus	Pale lilac	12cm (5in)
salzmanii	Lilac	10cm (4in)
sativus (Saffron)	Very large, rosy-lilac	10cm (4in)
speciosus and vars	Blue to lavender	12cm (5in)
zonatus	Pale lilac	10cm (4in)

Almost all crocuses have white or yellow throats.

Cyclamen cilicium	Pale rose	6cm (2½in)
hederifolium	Rose-pink or white	10cm (4in)
Galanthus reginae-olgae	White snowdrop with green markings	12cm (5in)
Sternbergia lutea	Yellow, crocus-like	12cm (5in)

The best are: *S. commixta* 'Embley', large clusters of orange-red; *S.c.* 'Jermyns', amber, becoming orange-red; *S. aucuparia* varieties, the longest-lasting of which is 'Fructu-luteo', whose berries are yellow; *S. vilmorinii*, red in late summer, becoming pink, then white with a pink flush; *S.* × *kewensis*, very large clusters of orange-red; *S.* 'Joseph Rock', amber-yellow, very long-lasting; *S. hupehensis*, white, dangling, lasting well into winter. Perhaps the longest-lasting red-berried sorbus is *S. esserteauana*, whose berries are rather small but still conspicuous.

Shrubs

Berried shrubs for autumn will be found in the genera *Aucuba*, *Berberis*, *Callicarpa*, *Chaenomeles*, *Clerodendrum*, *Cotoneaster*, *Euonymus*, *Gaultheria*, *Pernettya*, *Photinia*, *Pyracantha*, *Rosa*, *Sambucus*, *Skimmia*, *Symphoricarpos*, *Vaccinium* and *Viburnum*. There are too many species and varieties to list.

Roses provide perhaps the largest and most effective of all shrub fruit. Varieties of *Rosa rugosa*, and several of the species, notably *R. moyesii*, are worth seeking out for the long extension to their season given by their large, brilliant 'hips'.

bright orange seed in each wart. The seeds emerge and dangle for a short while on strings of mucus. That may all sound like a horror movie, but it is in fact very attractive.

Malus The crab apples are the best of all fruiting trees for this time of year. Many of them keep their fruits well past the end of next month; indeed, some persist right through the winter. *M.* 'Crittenden', sadly becoming scarce, is about the longest-lasting, with many, bright scarlet crab apples. Of the more readily available ones, 'Golden Hornet' is probably the best bet for quite large, bright yellow fruit retained through most of the winter, while 'John Downie' is the best crab apple of all, with large, orange-red fruit well beyond the New Year, from which, unlike most ornamental, long-lasting crabs, good jelly with a fine flavour can be made.

Sorbus This genus consists of the whitebeams and the mountain ashes, of which the latter provide the best fruit, usually seen as large clusters of berries in brilliant red, yellow or white. Most red berries are lost rapidly, soon after their formation in late summer, but those that remain, along with the white and yellow berries, will see the month through, if not persist well into winter.

NOVEMBER

November's sky is chill and drear
November's leaf is red and sear
SIR WALTER SCOTT

It is difficult to speak with dispassion of this time of year. To affect a false cheeriness and declare it to have effects on one's psyche other than those that are real would be to deny that it has any effect at all.

In the garden the memory of what was so recently rich with colour, scent and bustle is too fresh. I live in a maritime land, where it is almost unheard of for there to be significant snow this month, and there is no sudden transition, no brilliant carpeting of white, through which berries pierce like wine split upon a cloth of damask. There is just a running down, as if age had crept silently upon the garden and struck it with decrepitude.

And yet, as this weary month moves on, minutiae begin to register. Tiny-flowered asters, poor relations of the gaudy Michaelmas daisies, peep as if to ask if they can come out now.

Skimmias are wreathed in bud-clusters, the promise of spring. And there are berries.

Hydrangeas, their colour changes complete, change texture from their silkiness of late summer to a softness like that of finest kid. Above and among them, perhaps, the tall feathers of pampas grass stand guard.

Is there then no magic in late autumn? Of course there is. As when the sun returns one still afternoon and beams its way through the wisps of the morning's mist, setting flame to a liquidambar's ember-glowing leaves, slanting whitely across a birch's trunk, and picking out the crocuses, like amethysts on a tawny carpet.

Such moments are short, but full of poignancy. Perhaps that is the true spirit of this lonely month. Its treasures, when found, may be put away among the fondest memories.

tasks
FOR THE
month
1

PREVENT DAMAGE
Tie in any loose shoots of shrubs and climbers trained on walls and fences. They will be damaged by wind and themselves cause damage if left to flail about.

CHECKLIST

- Lift early-flowering border chrysanthemums
- Dry seedheads for winter arrangements
- Clean, sharpen and service garden tools and equipment
- Plant roses
- Finish planting tulips and plant hyacinths
- Plant containerised trees and shrubs
- Finish planting spring bedding and winter pansies
- After you have completed tidying and weeding around the herbaceous perennials, fork in bonemeal at 120gm per sq m (3½oz per sq yd)
- Continue to take hardwood cuttings

MAINTENANCE

BORDER CHRYSANTHEMUMS

Early-flowering border chrysanthemums should be lifted early this month. Cut the stems back to within 15cm (6in) of their bases and then wash all the soil off the roots. Place the plants in boxes of old compost or a mixture of peat and sand, water them well, and then let them overwinter in a dry, frost-free greenhouse.

SEEDHEADS

Although you will have been cutting back and tidying up among the border plants, it is worth remembering to leave attractive seedheads such as those of *Allium schubertii*. The longest-lasting of them are most intriguing when snowfall arrives, but if you do not want to leave them that long, hang them up to dry in a spare room for use in winter arrangements.

Don't forget that a few border plants such as *Iris foetidissima* have attractive seeds.

MAINTAINING TOOLS AND EQUIPMENT

Many, many gardeners find themselves caught out once this month is over. Next month has its own pressing preoccupations, and in no time at all you will be off and running again. There is no better time for looking after your garden tools and equipment. Unless they are in good condition, your garden will never have quite the well-groomed look that it should. Furthermore, the energy you will have to put into almost every operation will be considerably increased with blunt or corroded tools.

Clean and sharpen everything you can, oil them, and hang them neatly. Take secateurs, mowers and other machinery to be serviced and do not leave it until the last minute.

It is a temptation but a great mistake to leave tools outside. You should bring them in every night, otherwise wooden handles become roughened and uncomfortable (and less efficient) to use.

PLANTING

ROSES

Mail-order roses will be arriving about now and should be planted right away. However, if the weather is cold and wet, or the soil is just too wet for working, heel them in. This is just a matter of digging a trench at an angle away from the prevailing wind, in as sheltered a spot as you can find, and laying in the roses with their roots covered with a mixture of sand and moist peat.

■ Before planting, cut back any damaged roots to clean, undamaged wood.

■ Planting technique governs the future of roses more than almost anything else. The stiff, bare roots and prickly stems make roses feel tricky to handle, but the secret is to dig out a hole large enough for the roots to be properly spread. Do not make it too deep, but break up the bottom well.

■ Mix some of the good topsoil you have taken out with its own volume of thoroughly well-rotted organic matter – leaf-mould, garden compost or manure – or, if you have none, use peat to which you have added bonemeal at the rate of a double handful to the barrowload (two if you are a woman).

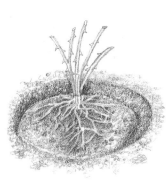

■ As you backfill, hold onto the stems and work them up and down with a jiggling motion to settle the soil among the roots.

■ When you finally firm the soil, its surface should be *just* above the bud union, which you can see as a thickening at the base of the plant.

■ All roses should be pruned fairly hard at planting time in order to promote bushy growth. This should not be too drastic, however, as frost may cause dieback and you do not want it to penetrate to the base. It is

better to return to the plants in early spring and take out any browned sections of stem.

PLANNING

● GARDEN PAPERWORK

Gardening involves quite a bit of clerical work, and we usually find ourselves too busy to attend to it during the warmer months. Some of us try everything to get out of such chores, but they should be done if you can, even though gardening may be but a favourite pastime. Here are some paperwork tasks for which this late autumn period is ideal:

■ Write to all the nurseries and seed houses whose catalogues you would like to receive and ask to be put on their mailing lists. They may put a charge on your first order for their catalogue, or they may reply asking you to send a small sum. Either of these practices is perfectly reasonable. Any firm, however, that fails to accord you the courtesy of a positive reply, is not worth dealing with.

■ Check your bookshelf. Are you missing information that you have found you need to have handy during the season?

■ Check your stocks of labels. Have you really got enough with which to start the next season? Don't forget, seed sowing starts in late winter. And have you enough pots and trays?

■ Take a trip to the garden centre and look at the new stock of practical items which are coming in now.

■ Now for the cherry on the pie. Bearing the above points

in mind, compile a list of items that you would like to receive from friends and loved ones as presents. A second list could, of course, consist of things you know would be appreciated as gifts from you.

■ This book is the result of many years of record keeping. I have kept my notebooks running and generally transferred their contents to files. This may seem to turn gardening into drudgery, but in fact has the opposite effect and makes it much easier. Most gardeners fail to appreciate that planning, planting and flowering are quite often widely separated events, and it is a major contribution to the quality of a garden if plants seen elsewhere are noted down for planting – even if it is only on a 'one day maybe' basis.

■ Although I have nagged about the virtues of keeping records and notes, it is probably only because I recognise in myself a somewhat less than well organised person, whose gardening successes would have been the fewer were it not for this self-imposed discipline.

■ How you arrange a gardening filing system will of course be a personal thing, but the main categories to start with are those used in these pages – monthly checklist, planting, planning and maintenance. Add to these a propagation schedule, a file for 'plants for the future', and one for cuttings from gardening magazines, and you will effectively begin to customise this book.

CLIMBING ROSES FOR SHADE

For a shady wall, try the following climbing roses:

'Danse du Feu' (orange-scarlet)
'Leverkusen' (creamy yellow)
'Madame Alfred Carrière' (creamy white)
'Maigold' (yellow)
'The New Dawn' (pink)
All of them are remarkably free from disease

PLANTING CLIMBING ROSES
Roses to grow on walls should be planted with their centres no less than 40cm (16in) from them.

plants
OF THE
month

ASTER
Aster ludoviciana var. *latifolia*

This late-flowering aster is rare in cultivation and not easy to obtain, but as interest in making the garden more attractive in late autumn and winter increases, it stands a good chance of becoming more accessible. Its clouds of little flowers are infinitely to be welcomed this month.

type	Herbaceous perennial
flowers	Sprays of small, lilac daisies
foliage	Slight, slender leaves
height	90cm (36in)
spread	1m (40in)
hardiness	Hardy
planting	Plant in spring
position	Sun or part shade
soil	Any good garden soil, preferably moisture retentive
propagation	By division in spring
alternatives	There are several small-flowered asters, notably the varieties of *A. ericoides*, but they flower earlier

SKIMMIA
Skimmia japonica

Nurserymen will tell you that it is not easy to sell plants with the sexes on separate individuals. With skimmias, although there is one exception, you need a male and a female if you are to see the brilliant, scarlet berries,

and people balk at having to buy two plants. They should not, though, as the male plants have a long-lasting beauty all of their own, with tight clusters of buds studding the bushes from autumn right through until flowering time in spring.

type	Evergreen shrub
flowers	Terminal panicles, usually white, mid- to late spring. Fragrant
fruit	Round, shiny, scarlet, very long-lasting berries, borne on female plants. *S.j.* subsp. *reevesiana* is hermaphrodite and all plants bear berries
foliage	Leathery, elliptic leaves
height	90–100cm (36–40in) after 10 years
spread	90–100cm (36–40in) after 10 years
hardiness	Hardy
position	Very useful shrubs for shady positions, but will also grow in sun
soil	Any reasonable garden soil, including chalk. *S.j. reevesiana*, however, is not tolerant of chalk soils
pruning	None
propagation	By semi-ripe cuttings in autumn in a cold frame, or in summer under mist
varieties	'Veitchii' (syn. 'Foremannii') is a vigorous female with large clusters of bright red fruits. 'Rubella' is a male with conspicuous clusters of dark red buds, which open to white flowers in spring

SKIMMIA JAPONICA

PHOTINIA
Photinia davidiana

Among the brightest of the berries that bring colour to the flower garden at its lowest ebb are those of *Photinia davidiana*. This plant was until recently a member of the genus *Stranvaesia*, which has now disappeared. Photinias are evergreen in the main, and some are grown for their fine, red young leaves. It is their berries, however, for which those that were stranvaesias are best known.

type	Evergreen shrub
flowers	White, in branched clusters in spring
fruits	Large clusters of bright red berries
foliage	Leathery, dark green, fairly slender
height	1.2m (4ft) after 10 years
spread	1m (4ft) after 10 years
hardiness	Hardy
position	Sun or part shade
soil	Any good garden soil. Please note that deciduous photinias are usually lime-hating
pruning	None
propagation	By semi-ripe cuttings under mist in late summer
alternatives	'Fructu-luteo' has bright yellow berries, 'Palette' is a singularly repellent form with leaves blotched and streaked with white. Unfortunately, it commands a considerable market

PAMPAS GRASS
Cortaderia selloana 'Sunningdale Silver'

Pampas grass is so well known as hardly to warrant description. However, it is not generally appreciated that there are several varieties of it, some of which are more suitable for small gardens than the more commonly seen tall ones. 'Sunningdale Silver' is of medium size but 'Pumila' is the variety that should be sought if pampas grass is to be in scale with the average garden.

type	Evergreen grass
flowers	Tall plumes of silvery white
foliage	Long, arching, grassy, sharp edged
height	2m (7ft)
spread	1.5m (5ft)
hardiness	Hardy
planting	Plant in late spring
position	Full sun
soil	Any reasonable garden soil
propagation	By division in late spring. It is not easy, and should be done without

PHOTINIA DAVIDIANA

CORTADERIA SELLOANA 'SUNNINGDALE SILVER'

	allowing the roots to become dry
alternatives	'Pink Feather' has a pinkish tinge to the flowers. 'Rendatleri' is praised for its lilac-pink plumes, but it is a very large plant up to 3m (10ft) tall

plants
IN
flower

PLEASE NOTE
All the above trees and shrubs flower intermittently over many weeks, often enjoying bursts of bloom as late as the end of winter. Mild spells of weather usually precede or coincide with flowering.

COTONEASTERS
Some of the best cotoneaster species for autumn colour, such as *C. lucidus*, are now uncommon in cultivation, probably because of the emphasis that has been laid on berries within the genus.

TREES	colour	flower type
Prunus subhirtella 'Autumnalis'	Pink	Small, like cherry blossom

SHRUBS		
Jasminum nudiflorum	Yellow	On bare branches
Viburnum × *bodnantense* vars	Light rose	In clusters, sweet scent
farreri	Pink	In clusters, highly scented

Erica carnea vars, including **'Myretoun Ruby', 'Pink Spangles', 'Foxhollow', 'Praecox Rubra', 'Ruby Glow', 'Vivellii', 'Springwood White'.**

CLIMBERS		
*Clematis cirrhosa balearica	Pale yellow, red spots	

PERENNIALS

Apart from *Schizostylis coccinea,* forms of which may flower on into this month, flowering of perennials, whether herbaceous or evergreen, has ceased.

BULBS	colour	height
Crocus clusii	Lilac	8cm (3in)
longiflorus	Large, lilac	10cm (4in) Scented
tournefortii	Lilac	10cm (4in)

TREES for autumn leaf colour	colour
Acer cappadocicum 'Rubrum'	Red, then gold
griseum	Crimson and scarlet
grosseri var. hersii	Yellow, then red
pensylvanicum	Butter yellow
rubrum 'October Glory	Flame red
rufinerve	Yellow
Amelanchier lamarckii	Orange and red
Betula spp	Most turn yellow
Crataegus × *lavallei*	Red
Ginkgo biloba	Yellow, but fall before this month
Koelreuteria paniculata	Yellow
Liquidambar styraciflua	Flame crimson
Liriodendron tulipifera	Gold
Malus spp and vars – some	Red and gold
Parrotia persica	Red, orange and yellow. Early
Prunus (Cherries) – most	Shades of yellow, orange or red
Sorbus spp – many	Shades of copper, red and orange

SHRUBS for autumn leaf colour

Acer japonicum 'Aconitifolium'	Rich crimson
'Aureum'	Golden leaves with little or no autumn colour
palmatum vars	There are currently approximately 150 of these Japanese maples. Virtually all have superb autumn colour, usually in bright yellow or intense, flame red
Azalea – deciduous	This branch of Rhododendron is one of the richest sources of autumn colour among shrubs. Colours vary from rich yellow to dazzling red
Berberis deciduous – many	Mostly red, some are orange
Callicarpa bodinieri vars	Violet-purple
Ceratostigma willmottianum	Purplish red
Cercidiphyllum japonicum	Pink, red and yellow
Cornus florida vars	Orange or scarlet
kousa chinensis	Brownish crimson
mas	Brownish red
Cotinus coggygria vars	Red
Cotoneaster adpressus	Scarlet
bullatus	Scarlet
divaricatus	Brilliant scarlet
horizontalis	Rich red
Enkianthus campanulatus	Yellow and red
Euonymus alatus	Bright scarlet
europaeus 'Red Cascade'	Rich scarlet
Fothergilla major	Mixed colours: orange, red, yellow on the same leaf
Hamamelis spp and vars	Most hamamelis colour richly in autumn. The majority turn yellow. **H. intermedia 'Jelena'** is particularly spectacular, in orange, scarlet and crimson
Nandina domestica	Red
Rhus typhina	Orange and red
Viburnum carlesii	Yellow
lantana	Crimson
opulus	Orange and red

CLIMBERS for autumn leaf colour

Parthenocissus spp	The most brilliant red hues of all
Vitis coignetiae	Orange and dark crimson
'Brandt'	Pink, orange and dark crimson

AUTUMN COLOURS

Autumn leaf colour is dependent on several factors, only very few of which are in the control of the gardener. The chief of these is wind. During a calm autumn, the leaves will stay for a long time on the trees provided they are not blown off by strong winds. Eventually, of course, the slightest breath will dislodge them, but in the earlier stages it takes more than a mere breeze.

If you shelter the best subjects, particularly the Japanese maples, which need shelter from wind in any case as part of their cultural requirements, the autumn colour in your garden will last much longer. That colour is important to you is implicit in the fact that you are reading this book; there is nothing we can do about the paucity of flowering in late autumn and winter beyond trying to grow the plants that do flower during the short days, but we can provide our gardens with colour by growing trees and shrubs that colour well during the earlier part of the season of sparse flowering.

However, it is a great mistake to take this too far. Autumn colour is at best fleeting; at worst, it hardly happens at all. It depends on climatic conditions and may be very poor in a year in which there is a cool summer and a mild autumn. Wherever those conditions obtain in most years, autumn colour is something for which you should not plant. In those circumstances, you should choose plants for their other virtues and take whatever autumn colour comes as a bonus. You are, if your climate is mild, more likely to enjoy long-lasting berries, as the birds will not become hungry as quickly as they do in climates where winter descends rapidly.

Gardens on acid soils enjoy better opportunities for autumn colour, as so many deciduous acid-loving plants do take on brilliant hues. It is not worth growing a deciduous azalea, for example, in a tub just for its autumn colour, but if it is part of a group of acid-loving plants grown in a large tub or a raised bed made with acid soil where the general garden soil is alkaline, then so much the better for the long-term attractiveness of the group.

DECEMBER

I dreamed that, as I wandered by the way,
Bare winter suddenly was changed to spring.
SHELLEY

*Poor Shelley! His superb imagination was able to banish winter,
and he could envisage 'pied windflowers and violets…faint
oxlips, tender bluebells…' but his dramatic nature would not let
him rest. He had to turn, stumbling from the scene, no doubt with
back of hand to tormented forehead, to show it to someone. 'Oh! to
whom?', was his mournful cry.*

*Midwinter is certainly a time for positive thinking. That, after
all, is the real reason for the timing of Christmas, which the early
church wisely placed in the way of the ancient festivals of midwinter. As gardeners, we could do much worse than emulate the
poet and dream of flowers yet to come. Only it goes without saying
that, as good gardeners, our dreaming will be translated into
planning, and our planning eventually into execution.*

*There are flowers out this month. The very last crocus, a
precocious snowdrop, and a little family of cyclamen snuggle
beneath trees or beside shrubs, while a handful of opportunist
shrubs bloom whenever there is a spell of settled, mild weather.*

*They do this in the 'hope' that the weather will also tempt
pollinating insects from hibernation for a short spell, and press
hard for their attention in most cases by being highly fragrant.
The middle of winter is no pageant of flowers, but it is fascinating
to see how nature is capable of fitting plants into every possible
ecological and climatic slot. It is easy to become inordinately fond
of the flowers of winter and to ascribe to them virtues which they
do not possess. We may think of them as brave, mainly because we
like to feel brave when we venture out of doors on cold days, but
they are not, of course. They are merely doing what all flowering
plants do – taking every opportunity to perpetuate their species.*

plants
OF THE
month

▼ HELLEBORE
Helleborus niger hybrid

Helleborus niger itself is the Christmas rose, whose large wide open, almost flat flowers, like white wheels, adorn cool, shady corners of the garden in winter. Often in the past, however, gardeners have found themselves with seedlings that were either poor forms of the species or haphazard hybrids with others. In more recent years, the Christmas rose has been deliberately crossed with other species, such as *H. corsicus* and *H. lividus*, and selections made of those with special qualities. Several are excellent, elegant, very early-flowering hellebores and valuable additions to the winter garden scene.

type	Partly evergreen perennials
flowers	Vary in colour and shape. They are usually borne in terminal clusters, and the individual flowers may droop to a greater or lesser degree before becoming more erect. Flower colour is usually based on white, greenish white, or white with a very faint pink flush, and the insides may be unmarked or faintly spotted or splashed. Flowering time varies, but is usually in mid to late winter
foliage	Also variable, but usually grey-green and tripartite
height	30cm (1ft)
spread	25cm (10in)
hardiness	Most are hardy
planting	Best in spring
position	Part shade
soil	A good, leafy, moisture-retentive soil
propagation	By division after flowering of large, well-established clumps only
alternatives	None, apart from *H. niger*
special comment	These plants generally circulate among keen gardeners, but can often be obtained from nurseries specialising in hellebores

HELLEBORUS NIGER HYBRID

MAHONIA
Mahonia × media 'Winter Sun'

The varieties of *Mahonia × media* are hybrids between *M. japonica* and *M. lomariifolia*. The former parent brings hardiness, wonderfully long racemes of flowers, scent, and magnificent, bold, pinnate leaves with holly-like leaflets. The latter contributes an increase in the numbers of leaflets, producing a more lacy effect, and clusters of many, boldly upright racemes of richer yellow. Although *M. lomariifolia* is on the tender side, the hybrids that have been selected for distribution are hardy. Some of the hybrids may be only slightly fragrant, but in 'Winter Sun' they are notably so.

type	Evergreen shrub
flowers	Many racemes of rich yellow, fragrant flowers
foliage	Long, pinnate, rigid leaves with spiny leaflets
height	1.8m (6ft) after 10 years
spread	1.8m (6ft) after 10 years
hardiness	Hardy, but protect from freezing winds
position	Best in part shade
soil	Any garden soil, including chalk
pruning	None
propagation	See page 135

alternatives	'Buckland' has fewer leaflets and longer, more spreading racemes; 'Charity' can grow very tall and may need cutting hard back to prevent its shooting up into two or three leafless poles. When well grown it is majestic, with leaves over 0.5m (20in) long and large, terminal clusters of very long racemes, closely packed with deep yellow, lightly scented flowers

VIBURNUM

Viburnum tinus 'French White'

Viburnum tinus is the well-known laurustinus, unaccountably one of the most popular of all shrubs. One expresses surprise because it is rare for a winter-flowering shrub to catch the attention of the wider gardening public. It is, however, almost indestructible and one of the few evergreens that succeed when exposed to winds from the sea.

type	Evergreen shrub
flowers	Flat clusters of small, white flowers, produced almost continuously from autumn to spring
foliage	Tightly massed, glossy, dark green leaves
fruits	Black, small
height	1.5m (5ft) after 10 years
spread	1.5m (5ft) after 10 years
hardiness	Hardy
position	Sun or shade
soil	Any reasonable soil
pruning	None. Can be trimmed, after flowering to form a hedge
propagation	By semi-ripe cuttings in late summer to early autumn; root earlier ones under mist, later cuttings in a garden frame
alternatives	'Eve Price', buds carmine, flowers pink; 'Gwenllian', compact, deep pink in the bud, opening to white flowers with pink-backed petals

CYCLAMEN

Cyclamen coum

The botanists are not quite agreed on the status of this cyclamen. Some regard it as a species with several naturally occurring varieties, others as more or less an aggregate of species. From a gardener's point of view, it is a group of cyclamen capable of providing flowers from midwinter to early spring with a variety of colours based on carmine and including white forms, and with round leaves that may be plain green, marked with silver, or even completely silver.

type	Tuberous perennial
flowers	More truncated than other cyclamen and with the lobes arranged more sideways-on, sometimes giving the appearance of minute ships' propellers
foliage	Glossy to matt, silver to plain green, in most forms maroon on the undersides
height	10cm (4in)
spread	10cm (4in)
hardiness	Hardy
planting	Best purchased 'in the green' in spring from specialist nurseries and planted immediately
position	Part shade
soil	Any good garden soil, preferably leafy or otherwise organic
propagation	From seed sown immediately the pods split
varieties	There are several, but the names given are often contradictory. Choose from the catalogue the ones that will give you a good range of flowering times, colours and foliage

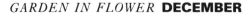

tasks

FOR THE

month

2

WARNING
Do not be tempted to take a short cut by saddle-grafting camellias. It is a method for stocks and scions of the same diameters and you might think it would save you a year or two on the growth of the rootstock. This is logical, but unfortunately saddle grafting is only satisfactory for camellias in the hands of a really experienced professional propagator

**TREES AND SHRUBS
FOR GRAFTING**

Cherry
Hawthorn
Maple
Robinia
Sorbus

PROPAGATION

GRAFTING

Camellia reticulata varieties are as different from other camellias as limousines are from good family cars. They have very large, frilled or wavy-petalled flowers in sumptuous shades of strawberry, but are quite tender. In comparatively recent years they have been hybridised with other species to produce hardier camellias with the same flower characteristics. They appear to be on the threshold of genuine popularity and can be grown where there is much frost but also reliable shelter from cold winds.

Unfortunately, they are not very easy to grow from cuttings. *C. reticulata* cannot be propagated this way at all, and its varieties vary from difficult to impossible, and even the easiest require the use of a mist propagation unit. When you are faced with the purchase of a rather expensive plant, of whose toleration of conditions in your garden you may not be too sure, it is highly likely finally to put you off if you hear that you may not be able to propagate it as insurance against its loss.

However, you may change your mind when you learn that these camellias *can* be grafted. Grafting is little done by amateurs but is not difficult, although it requires some manual dexterity. This is the ideal time to graft camellias and, although they will take up room in a heated frame or propagator, it will be during those few weeks between now and when you will need it for sowing seed.

Method
The method used for camellias is called 'spliced side-veneer grafting'. Like all other methods, it involves joining a rootstock (the stock) of one plant with a shoot (the scion) of another, by bringing the growing tissues under the barks of each into contact. It is a method particularly used when the stock stem is of larger diameter than that of the scion.

■ The stock should be a strong, pot-grown plant of any variety of *Camellia japonica*. It should be three to four years old at least. It is much better to prepare your own stock in advance from a cutting, as it takes some doing to decapitate (as you must) a plant for which you have paid good money. Bring it into a greenhouse or frame with an operating temperature of 8°C (46°F) or above so that growth may just be starting.

■ Your scion will be a 10cm (4in) shoot of this year's growth of your reticulata hybrid or form of the species. To prepare the stock to receive it, cut about 5mm (¼in) into its stem at a position as low as you can manage, and at a downward angle of about 45°. Now make a slanting cut from about 3cm (1¼in) above the first so that it meets it. Remove the sliver of wood.

■ Next, take the scion and, cutting on the slant towards its base, take off a shaving the same length as the sliver you removed from the stock. Cut the base of the scion at 45° to fit the lip of the stock.

■ Bring the two together so that there is a good, snug fit and the cut surfaces meet each other as much as possible, and bind them together firmly with raffia. There is no need to use grafting wax, as you next put the entire graft into a heated propagating frame. Around 15°C (59°F) will be the best temperature. The atmosphere should be humid to prevent water loss from the scion before union takes place.

■ This should happen in about six to eight weeks. You can tell by a general freshening of the appearance of the foliage of the scion and the start of new shoots. Remove the raffia. Cut the top of the stock at a point just above the union, taking care to cut cleanly and with no pulling. You can now harden off your new plant.

It goes without saying that the tools (knife and secateurs) you use must be keenly sharp. If you have used the secateurs for pruning camellias at any time, use another pair, as a nasty virus that causes yellow mottling of the leaves, to which *C. reticulata* is vulnerable, may have lurked in the sap of other camellias that are reasonably resistant to it. One grafted plant of mine, carelessly operated on with my regular pruning secateurs, was after ten years nothing more than a stunted mass of badly yellowed leaves.

BRANCHING OUT

Once you have mastered this off-season grafting method, you can try all the other fascinating types of grafting, including 'saddle-grafting' the larger rhododendrons, which looks easy but usually fails in inexperienced hands. The attraction is that you can grow the stocks (*Rhododendron ponticum*) quickly from seed.

Other trees and shrubs with which amateur gardeners can enjoy this most satisfying way of propagating are maples, hawthorns, cherries, robinias and *Sorbus* varieties.

TREES	colour	flower type
Prunus subhirtella **'Autumnalis'**	White	Semi-double
'Autumnalis Rosea'	White, blushed pink	Semi-double

SHRUBS		
Erica* × *darleyensis vars	Pink, rose, magenta or white	Heathers
Hamamelis × **intermedia** some vars	Yellow, bronze, copper or red	Spidery, held closely on bare branches
mollis vars	Shades of yellow	As above
Lonicera fragrantissima	Cream, fragrant	Tubular
× **purpusii**	Cream, fragrant	Tubular
'Winter Beauty'	As above	As above, free-flowering
standishii	White, tinged pink, fragrant	Tubular
***Mahonia* × *media* vars**	Yellow, fragrant	
Viburnum tinus	White or pink	In flat heads

Also: **Erica carnea** vars, **jasminum nudiflorum**, **Viburnum** × **bodnantense** vars, **Viburnum farreri**.

CLIMBERS		
Clematis cirrhosa balearica	Pale yellow, with red spots	

BULBS	colour	height
Crocus laevigatus fontanayi	Violet-blue	8cm (3in)
Cyclamen coum aggregate	Carmine to white	10cm (4in)
Galanthus corcyrensis	White, green markings	8cm (3in)

plants
IN
flower

PLEASE NOTE
Flowering may be delayed in many cases if the weather is particularly cold, and most of the plants listed may be in flower at any time between now and early spring.

VIBURNUM TINUS 'FRENCH WHITE.'

USEFUL ADDRESSES

UNITED KINGDOM
NURSERIES AND GARDEN CENTRES

Hillier Nurseries (Winchester) Ltd.,
Ampfield House, Ampfield,
Romsey, Hampshire SO51 9PA

Largest selection of trees and shrubs

Starborough Nursery,
Starborough Road,
Marsh Green,
Edenbridge, Kent TN8 5RB

Hardy and unusual trees and shrubs

Knap Hill & Slocock Nurseries,
Barrs Land, Knaphill,
Woking, Surrey GU21 2JW

Rhododendrons and azaleas

Four Seasons,
Forncett St. Mary, Norwich,
Norfolk NR16 1JT

Herbaceous perennials (mail order only)

Blooms of Bressingham Ltd,
Diss, Norfolk IP22 2AB

Herbaceous perennials, alpines, conifers, shrubs,
ornamental grasses

The Valley Clematis Nursery,
Hainton, Lincoln LN3 6LN

Clematis

Broadleigh Gardens,
Bishops Hull, Taunton,
Somerset TA4 1AE

Small bulbs, hostas, Pacific Coast irises

De Jagers,
Marden, Kent TN12 9BP

Bulbs, general

Inshriach Alpine Plant Nursery,
Inshriach, Aviemore,
Inverness-shire,
Scotland

Alpines and woodland plants

CLUBS AND ASSOCIATIONS

The Alpine Garden Society,
AGS Centre,
Avon Bank,
Pershore,
Worcestershire WR10 3JP

The Royal Horticultural Society,
80 Vincent Square,
London SW1P 2PE

The Hardy Plant Society,
Little Orchard,
Great Comberton,
Near Pershore,
Worcestershire WR10 3DP

USEFUL ADDRESSES

USA
NURSERIES AND GARDEN CENTRES

The Greenery,
1451 County Road 616,
Maple City,
Michigan 49664

Hardiest rhododendrons and kalmias

Roslyn Nursery,
Box 69, Roslyn,
New York 11576

Hardy plants; rhododendrons, azaleas, camellias, conifers, trees, shrubs, perennials

---

Lilypons Water Gardens,
PO Box 10, Buckeystown,
Maryland 21717

Water lilies

Siskyou Rare Plant Nursery,
2825 Cummings Road,
Medford,
Oregon 97501

Alpines, ferns and perennials

CLUBS AND ASSOCIATIONS

For information on 9,286 garden clubs in 50 States and the District of Columbia

The National Council of State Garden Clubs Inc.,
4401 Magnolia Avenue, St Louis,
Missouri 63110

For information on hardy plants

The Hardy Plant Society,
124 N. 181st Street, Seattle,
Washington 98133

American Horticultural Society,
Box 0105, Mount Vernon,
Virginia 22121

CANADA

C.A. Cruickshank Ltd.,
1015 Mount Pleasant Road,
Toronto, Ontario M4P 2MI

Bulbs

FURTHER READING

The Hillier Manual of Trees and Shrubs (David & Charles 1991 Edition).
Perennial Garden Plants Graham Stuart Thomas, in association with the Royal Horticultural Society (Dent, Revised, 1990).
The Heritage of the Rose David Austin (Antique Collectors Club, Revised, 1990).
Shrubs Through The Seasons Roy Lancaster (Harper Collins, 1991).
A Garden For All Seasons (Reader's Digest, 1991).
The All-Seasons Garden John Kelly (Frances Lincoln (UK), Viking (US), 1987).
Plants With Impact John Kelly (David & Charles, 1992).

INDEX

INDEX